a GRAND MOTHER'S prayers

60 days of devotions and prayer

kay swatkowski

Discovery House.
from Our Daily Bread Ministries

A Grandmother's Prayers: 60 Days of Devotions and Prayer

© 2015 by Kay Swatkowski

Discovery House is affiliated with Our Daily Bread Ministries, Grand Rapids, Michigan.

ISBN 978-1-62707-189-5

Printed in the United States of America

First printing in 2015

To Nicole, Kevin, Samantha, Madelyn,
and Holden.
You fill each day with love, laughter, and joy.
I am praying for you.

"I have no greater joy than to hear that my children
are walking in the truth."

3 John 1:4

To
Martha
Johnson
2015

From: aunt Sarah
Stanley & Edward

CONTENTS

ACKNOWLEDGMENTS

For more than three decades, I have grown in my belief in the necessity and importance of praying for our children and grandchildren. I am convinced that our prayers are the greatest gift we give them. Thank you to all of the kind, supportive, and talented people who have helped me put into words what I have been learning about prayer.

I thank my loving and ever-supportive husband, Ray, for cheering me on and encouraging me to put my thoughts on paper. Thank you to Jen, Rich, Jon, Lindy, Julie, Justin, Joy, and Tim for your love, encouragement, kindness, and patience with my questions and for always being interested. Thank you to Nicole, Kevin, Samantha, Madelyn, and Holden for reminding me of how much joy and satisfaction grandchildren can bring.

A heartfelt thank-you to my sisters Susan, Lisa, and Erin for sharing in the wonderful memories of our grandparents. I know you join me in thanking our grandparents for the kindness and generosity they extended to us each day.

Thank you to the families of Faith Church of Grayslake, Illinois. Observing as you have lovingly raised your children for Christ has been a memorable and inspiring experience. Thank you to Pastor Zack Turner. Your faithfulness to God's Word and your ability to bring truth into everyday life have encouraged our family and inspired many of this book's chapters.

A special thank you to Cheryl Tanner, Cheryl Moeller, Sherry Parmelee, Bev Puzia, Kelsie Newbrough, Laura Wintory, and Nancy Good for prodding me on and encouraging me in this process. You are wonderful friends. Without you, these stories would never have been written.

INTRODUCTION

Be silly. Be honest. Be kind.
Ralph Waldo Emerson

Metal lockers slammed as the chatter of children filled the hallway. Breathless boys and girls with dangling shoelaces scooted to water fountains. Lingering outside the classroom to soak up the fading moments of recess, all but one of my first-grade students dawdled.

Blue-eyed Katianna screeched down the hall to greet me, gym shoes squealing and blond hair flying. Wrapping thin arms around me and squeezing tight, she giggled and declared, "Mrs. Swatkowski, you are just the right kind of squishy for hugging."

Katianna's affectionate comment reminded me of an important truth. Children care little about our appearance. Our age, profession, or social status does not matter to them at all.

Their needs are simple.

Children long for warm, generous, respectful, loving relationships with the big people in their world. They crave adult relationships that provide kindness and reassurance. They long for our time, patience, and attention.

Sadly, the silly, fun-loving, caring adult friendship every child hungers for is a casualty of our culture's hurried attitude toward life. Grandparents, time-honored leisurely companions and gentle guides for grandchildren, often bear weighty and consuming concerns of their own and find their time and energy limited.

Their influence is profoundly missed. Children seem to be the biggest losers in our speed-oriented, achievement-addicted culture.

In this overscheduled, high-pressure environment, children benefit more than ever from a close relationship with their grandparents. Research reveals that the love and care of the older generation has a positive impact on children in many ways. One study found a definite link between grandparent involvement and adolescent well-being. Grandparents provide not only affection and support, but also wisdom, problem-solving, and stability during times of family crisis.

God is not finished with us. We have a critical job to do.

Many grandparents live hundreds or even thousands of miles away from their grandchildren and are not able to be as involved as they would like. Health issues can limit the participation of grandparents who live nearby. Other grandparents provide daily care for grandchildren and struggle to balance their love for and commitment to their grandchildren with the personal concerns that accompany this stage of life. For some, there are financial or relational considerations that make connecting with grandchildren complicated.

Whatever our situation, there is one thing we all can do for our grandchildren. We can pray. Whether near or far, we can be engaged in the lives of our grandchildren and be connected to them in the most caring of ways—through prayer.

"I wandered away from the church during my teen years but always knew my grandmother loved me and was praying for me."

"I know that I am a Christian today because of my grand-mother's prayers."

"My family life was chaotic, but the love of my grandparents provided the stability I needed to survive."

During my years spent working in women's ministry, I con-stantly heard women affectionately sharing stories like these of the love, support, and prayers of their grandparents and the effect of these relationships on their Christian life. The care and prayer of grandparents can make all the difference. I invite you to join me in praying for our grandchildren. As best you can, use this guide for sixty consecutive days, choosing one or two of the prayer suggestions at the end of each devotional, or pick up this book from time to time to concentrate on one area of need.

It is my prayer that A Grandmother's Prayers will be a source of encouragement to you as you bring your cherished grandchildren before God. May it be a reminder to you of the important role you play in the emotional and spiritual lives of children.

day one:
ONE ENDLESS LINE OF FAITH

I ask God most often that we would be an unbroken line of Christians until Christ returns.

A Grandfather's Prayer

The true worshipers will worship the Father in the Spirit and in truth, for they are the kind of worshipers the Father seeks.

John 4:23

The sign at the entrance that instructed worshipers to observe silence was written in four languages. A steady stream of hushed and compliant sightseers from every corner of the world tiptoed through Notre Dame Cathedral in Paris—past flickering, smoldering candles, shaky wooden chairs, massive stone pillars, and worn-out kneelers.

We paused partway through the cathedral at a small, antiquated wooden door. Less than six feet high, the deteriorating door marked one of the first entrances to an early version of the cathedral, dating back to about AD 1200. Natural light streaming through the famed Rose Windows danced across the cold, gray stone floor in faint shades of blue and red. We reverently walked behind the altar. That afternoon, a service was being conducted in German.

Impressive? Unforgettable? Beautiful? Awe-inspiring? Yes.

However, it was not the architecture, the symbolic windows, or the artwork that touched my heart. It was the floor.

As we wandered through one of the most famous cathedrals in the world, holding the hands of our four children, I noticed what seemed to be a path that had been worn into that ancient floor. For the nearly eight centuries before our family ever set foot in the cathedral, thousands upon thousands of others had circled that altar, just as we had. Most came longing to find God, wanting to serve Him, desperate to know Him.

In that moment, I understood as never before that my husband and I, as well as our four children, were part of an endless line of Christians. We were among those who were seeking to know and love God. We were walking a holy path traveled by millions before us.

Today we yearn for our grandchildren to be a part of that endless line of Christians. Inviting them to participate in this lineage of faith is the greatest calling we have. At whatever level we are able to share the faith our family members' hold dear, it is an honor and a privilege to be part of the spiritual formation that can take place in a home.

So where do we begin?

Let us pray that our families will embrace Christ and indeed continue that one endless line of faith until He returns. Let us also pray that God will work tenderness into our own hearts as we walk hand in hand with our children and grandchildren so they too will join us as our brothers and sisters in Christ.

Let Us Pray That . . .

- we grandparents worship in Spirit and truth (John 4:23).

- we take seriously our role as communicators of the faith (Deuteronomy 4:9).

- we communicate our faith with gentleness and respect (Philippians 4:5).

- we will be humble and nonjudgmental and will at all times honor the role of our grandchildren's parents (Ephesians 4:2).

- our grandchildren's hearts will cherish our spiritual heritage (Proverbs 1:8).

- every member of our family will be part of the endless line of faith (3 John 1:4).

Heavenly Father, I come to you in gratitude for the grandchildren you have blessed us with. They are a gift that reminds me of the joys that come with the very act of living. My deepest desire and most earnest prayer is that these children will become Christ-followers. Help me, Lord, to be faithful in modeling the life of a Christ-follower and in praying that my family would be part of the endless line of Christians. Amen.

Think and Do

- Read Deuteronomy 4:9. What new insights does this verse give you into the role of grandparents in communicating spiritual truth?
- Were you blessed to receive a spiritual heritage? What stories of your spiritual heritage can you share with your grandchildren?
- Are you a first-generation Christian, or can you trace your faith back a few generations? Do you have any pictures of family members who have passed their faith on to you? Spend an afternoon sharing memories of these special people with your grandchildren. You may be the only link they have to their spiritual heritage.

"Yet a time is coming and has now come when the true worshipers will worship the Father in the Spirit and in truth, for they are the kind of worshipers the Father seeks" (John 4:23).

"Only be careful, and watch yourselves closely so that you do not forget the things your eyes have seen or let them fade from your heart as long as you live. Teach them to your children and to their children after them" (Deuteronomy 4:9).

"Let your gentleness be evident to all. The Lord is near" (Philippians 4:5).

"Be completely humble and gentle; be patient, bearing with one another in love" (Ephesians 4:2).

"I have no greater joy than to hear that my children are walking in the truth" (3 John 1:4).

day two:
KIND WORDS

Kind words can be short and easy to speak, but their echoes are truly endless.

Mother Teresa

Gracious words are a honeycomb, sweet to the soul and healing to the bones.

Proverbs 16:24

Set in Mississippi at the time of the birth of the civil rights movement in the United States, Kathryn Stockett's novel *The Help* touches on a number of heart-rending themes. The main character, Aibileen Clark, served white families all her adult life. While cooking, cleaning, and doing laundry for these families, she raised and loved seven children as if they were her own. As the story opens, the wise and gentle woman is caring for toddler Mae Mobley.

Aibileen adored and worried over Mae. Little Mae loved her Aibileen.

One morning, she gathered the girl onto her lap in a rocking chair. Tenderly and with great delight, Aibileen looked into her eyes and whispered, "You is kind. You is smart. You is important."[1]

In 1993, John Trent and Gary Smalley collaborated on a book considered by many to be a classic: *The Blessing*. Using the Bible and personal experience, the authors describe the unconditional love and acceptance that every child craves. Research and their own understanding of family dynamics led the authors to believe there are five essential components for communicating unconditional love and acceptance—the blessing—to the waiting hearts of children and grandchildren:

- Meaningful touch
- A spoken message
- Attaching high value
- Picturing a special future
- An active commitment[2]

Aibileen Clark gave Mae a blessing. Meaningful touch, spoken words, communicating high value, picturing a future, and an active commitment to this little girl's welfare were all part of this powerful interaction.

My husband and I frequently spend Fridays with our three youngest grandchildren: Samantha, Madelyn, and Holden. Playing hide-and-seek or princess, making pretend cookies from Play-Doh, sharing ice-cream cones, and going for walks occupy most of our day.

One of their favorite activities is to climb all over Grandpa as if he were a jungle gym at the park. As they climb and tumble and squeal, it is like watching a litter of puppies. It's the best day of the week.

On a recent Friday, I whispered to the five-year-old, "Samantha, you are beautiful." She smiled. Then, remembering Aibileen's example, I added, "And you are kind."

With surprise she asked, "I am kind?"

"Yes. You are kind." After a hug and a kiss she skipped off to find Grandpa. However, it was evident to me that my simple words had reached her five-year-old heart.

As a grandparent, I have the honor of assuring my grandchildren of my unconditional love and acceptance. Passing a blessing to my grandchild can be as simple as sharing tender words that encourage and affirm.

I pray that the Lord will remind me to speak to my grandchildren with tenderness and insight. I pray that they will look back on their childhood remembering Grandma's words of blessing.

Let Us Pray That . . .

- we take advantage of every opportunity to give a blessing to our grandchildren (Numbers 6:24–26).
- we show affection to our grandchildren (Matthew 19:14–15).
- we learn how to use our words to bless our grandchildren (Proverbs 16:21).
- we assure our grandchildren that God has prepared a future for them (Jeremiah 29:11).
- we become as actively engaged in our grandchildren's lives as is appropriate and as we are able.

Loving Father, I thank you for the assurance and blessing of your tender and unconditional love. Every day you bless my life with your love and promises. Lord, make my sometimes hurried and preoccupied heart sensitive to my grandchildren's eagerness to receive a blessing from our family. Help me to understand their unique temperaments and needs, and communicate love and acceptance to them in ways that speak to their hearts. Let my kind words be an endless echo in their lives. May they not only receive a blessing from me but may they also experience the blessing of being your children. Amen.

Think and Do

- You may want to get a copy of John Trent's *Bedtime Blessings* to read to your grandchildren as you tuck them in to sleep at your house.
- Write a special prayer of blessing for each grandchild, being especially careful to attach high value and picture a special future.
- If you did not receive a blessing from your own parents, *The Blessing* may offer you some help in recovering from that loss. The Lord has a blessing for you (Zephaniah 3:17).

"The LORD bless you and keep you; the LORD make his face shine on you and be gracious to you; the LORD turn his face toward you and give you peace" (Numbers 6:24–26).

"Jesus said, 'Let the little children come to me, and do not hinder them, for the kingdom of heaven belongs to such as these.' When he had placed his hands on them, he went on from there" (Matthew 19:14–15).

"The wise in heart are called discerning, and gracious words promote instruction" (Proverbs 16:21).

" 'For I know the plans I have for you,' declares the LORD, 'plans to prosper you and not to harm you, plans to give you hope and a future' " (Jeremiah 29:11).

day three:
THE JESUS SONG

Though our feelings come and go, God's love for us does not.

C. S. Lewis

See what great love the Father has lavished on us, that we should be called children of God! And that is what we are!

1 John 3:1

Smelling of soap and shampoo and dressed in his warm and cozy green flannel pajamas dotted with parading duckies, he was too adorable to refuse. Eventually, my attempts to leave his room met with emotional protests of "Grandma, I'm afraid to be alone." Followed by "I need another drink of water."

Switching on the nightlight and offering comforting words, I attempted a stealth tactic: I tried to quietly back out of the room.

My sly efforts were wholly derailed when my grandson pleaded, "Grandma, would you sing the Jesus song?" Sitting beside Kevin, I tucked him in once more and began to sing: "Jesus loves me, this I know; for the Bible tells me so. Little ones to Him belong; they are weak, but He is strong." In a matter of minutes, our grandson had rolled over and drifted into a peaceful sleep.

When asked in his later years to share the most meaningful truth of his life, the great theologian Karl Barth replied, "Jesus loves me, this I know."[3]

Whether you are an aging theologian or a child just beginning life's journey, the knowledge of God's love is the soul's surest anchor.

Too many adolescents are searching for their identity through appearance, fashion, accomplishments, sports, grades, or peer acceptance. Some even turn to drugs and alcohol because those things help them find acceptance with others who are struggling in the same way.

These are flimsy things upon which to build an identity. When these weak substitutes collapse under our young people, the disappointment can be unbearable.

God's love is never changing. It is eternal. It is infinite. It is sure. It will never, ever disappoint.

In the same way that the apostle Paul prayed for the Ephesians, we can pray for our grandchildren. May they know how "wide and long and high and deep is the love of Christ" (Ephesians 3:18).

God's love is the source of their identity. Their self-worth comes from knowing they are deeply loved children. Self-confidence comes from knowing He made them for a purpose.

God's love will never disappoint them.

The most important truth our grandchildren will ever need to know is this: *Jesus loves me, this I know.*

Let Us Pray That . . .

- our grandchildren grasp and believe in the love of God for them (Ephesians 3:17–19).

- our grandchildren will be in awe of God's limitless love (Psalm 103:11).

- our grandchildren's belief in the unconditional love of God will be the starting place for their identity (1 John 3:1).

- our grandchildren delight themselves in the love of God (Psalm 13:5; Zephaniah 3:17).

- our grandchildren believe the Jesus song and offer it to others (Psalm 59:17).

Loving Father, I am overjoyed that your lavish love has declared me to be a child of God. What an honor to be your daughter. It is my heart's cry that each of my grandchildren will allow their roots to sink deeply into the rich soil of your infinite love. May your affection and care nourish and strengthen them in disappointment. May they shift their focus from their circumstances and onto your unfailing and dependable love. I ask, Father, that they would recognize that human worth and value come from the dignity you have bestowed upon each person and not from performance or the evaluation of other people. May your love be their strength and song. Amen.

Think and Do

- Read Romans 8:35. In difficult times, have you ever felt separated from the love of God? How true is it that you have been separated from His love? Is it 20 percent true, 50 percent true, 90 percent true? Or is it not true at all?

- Do you sense that your grandchildren sometimes base their value on their appearance or performance? How can you encourage your grandchildren in the steadfast love of God?

- From your own life, what story of God's love can you share with your grandchildren?

- Read Max Lucado's children's book *Just in Case You Ever Wonder* and use it as a springboard for talking about your unconditional love for your grandchild. Remind them of the even greater love of God.

"And I pray that you, being rooted and established in love, may have power together with all the Lord's holy people, to grasp how wide and long and high and deep is the love of Christ, and to know this love that surpasses knowledge— that you may be filled to the measure of all the fullness of God" (Ephesians 3:17–19).

"For as high as the heavens are above the earth, so great is his love for those who fear him" (Psalm 103:11).

"See what great love the Father has lavished on us, that we should be called children of God! And that is what we are!" (1 John 3:1).

"But I trust in your unfailing love; my heart rejoices in your salvation" (Psalm 13:5).

"The LORD your God is with you, the Mighty Warrior saves. He will take great delight in you; in his love he will no longer rebuke you, but will rejoice over you with singing" (Zephaniah 3:17).

"You are my strength, I sing praise to you; you, God, are my fortress, my God on whom I can rely" (Psalm 59:17).

day four:
THE SHADOW OF PROTECTION

Our safe place is not where we live, but in whom we live.

Tom White

Whoever dwells in the shelter of the Most High will rest in the shadow of the Almighty.

Psalm 91:1

It was a hot Fourth of July in 2001. I soaked my hot, tired feet in the ice-cold water of the kiddy pool, while our eighteen-month-old, sunblock-coated grandson Kevin splashed and played there. As I watched him, I was amused to see our adult son Jonathan circling Kevin in the little pool like a hawk.

Later, as we recalled the day's events, Jon explained his unusual behavior. "I was casting a shadow so Kevin wouldn't get sunburned."

Less than three weeks before, our son-in-law—Kevin's daddy—had lost his life in a motorcycle accident. Over those three weeks, we had grieved and prayed continually for God's protection and care for our daughter, granddaughter, and grandson.

Jonathan's words were a vivid picture of Psalm 91:1: "Whoever dwells in the shelter of the Most High will rest in the shadow of the Almighty."

When we are facing the most difficult moments of life and seek our shelter in God, He casts a shadow over our lives, protecting us from the things that would harm us most. Much of the time, we are as unaware of His loving presence and protection as Kevin was of his uncle's love and care. Yet God is always present, circling our lives, intently watching, caring, and inviting us to rest in the shadow He provides.

Every devoted parent and grandparent prays for God's protection and care for their children and grandchildren. Concerns for their health, safety, and future keep us up at night. As we pace the floor, we wrestle with how little power we have to protect them from disappointments and harm.

Prayer is the best answer for our concerns. As we pray, let us remember Psalm 91 and God's promise to hide us and our grandchildren in the shadow of His wings.

My prayer is that my grandchildren will seek protection there.

Let Us Pray That . . .

- our grandchildren choose to run to God for safety (Psalm 18:2).
- God provides protection and shelter for each of our grandchildren (Psalm 5:11).
- our grandchildren find emotional and spiritual rest in the shadow of the Almighty (Psalm 36:7).
- our grandchildren consistently turn to God alone for refuge and safety (Psalm 2:12).
- we are examples of people who turn to God for safety and security.
- we find natural opportunities to share stories of ways God has cared for us personally, even when we were unaware (Psalm 66:16).

Loving Protector, you are our refuge and shield. You are our hiding place and strong tower. When we face danger, we run to you for safety. Thank you for the protection you have given to our family day after day. My prayer, dear Lord, is that my grandchildren will turn to you alone for protection and care. I ask that their hearts would find peace and rest as they run to you for refuge and shelter. Hide them in the shadow of your wings. Amen.

Think and Do

- Read Psalm 121:1–2. Where does your help come from?
- Do you have stories of God's protection and care for you? Do you have a story of how God's presence strengthened you and helped at a moment of grief or loss?
- If possible, share a story of God's protection for your grandchildren when they were very young.
- Read the children's book *God Is with You* by Larry Libby to reinforce the concept of God's care in your grandchild's daily life.
- Suggest that your grandchildren help you choose a family verse that talks of God's love and care. Allow them to use their creativity and imagination to illustrate this verse. Have it framed, and allow the children to decide where to hang it in your home.

"The LORD is my rock, my fortress and my deliverer; my God is my rock, in whom I take refuge" (Psalm 18:2).

"But let all who take refuge in you be glad; let them ever sing for joy" (Psalm 5:11).

"How priceless is your unfailing love, O God! People take refuge in the shadow of your wings" (Psalm 36:7).

"Blessed are all who take refuge in him" (Psalm 2:12).

"Come and hear, all you who fear God; let me tell you what he has done for me" (Psalm 66:16).

day five:
IT IS NOT ABOUT YOU

I don't know what your destiny will be, but one thing I know;
the only ones among you who will be really happy are those
who will have sought and found how to serve.

Albert Schweitzer

But I am among you as one who serves.

Luke 22:27

Whether washing windows in a nursing home, praying for an emotionally wounded friend, or pulling rusty nails from deteriorating shingles in 90-degree heat with her youth group friends, our fourteen-year-old granddaughter Nicole seems to have grasped this concept.

From the time she was small, she has had a desire to help people. Nikki was born to love and serve. Groups such as Kids Against Hunger, Feed My Starving Children, and organizations that dig wells in Africa have captured her attention. Nikki is often more aware of compassionate ministries than I am.

Nikki's giving attitude also shapes her approach to money. Recently, before a much-anticipated concert, I wanted to slip Nikki some cash—to which she countered, "No, Grandma. I want to earn it."

It is promising to see young people willing to work hard, eager to extend themselves beyond their own hectic existence, prepared to take on the concerns of others and to serve.

Last summer, as Nicole worked with a local youth missions project, she became friends with young people from China. Her experience with another culture was rewarding. Like so many of her friends, she has a heart for the world. Teaching English as a Second Language may be in her future.

Our homes, our society, and our churches hinge upon the next generation's capacity to be compassionate, unselfish, honest, hardworking, moral, generous, and free of favoritism.

I am proud of my granddaughter. I am proud of her friends. They challenge me to renew my commitment to simply serve.

She gives me great hope for the future. We need to pray that the hearts of our grandchildren will not become hardened by life and material possessions and that they will grow in their desire to serve.

Let Us Pray That . . .

- our grandchildren will have tender hearts toward the hurting people of the world (Ephesians 4:32).

- as our grandchildren mature, they will learn not to show favoritism in any way (James 2:1).

- our grandchildren develop the capacity to empathize with, and be generous to, those in need (1 Timothy 6:18).

- our grandchildren have the opportunity to experience the joy of serving (Ephesians 6:7).

- our grandchildren will have discernment in serving and learn to serve in emotionally healthy ways (Philippians 2:3).

- our grandchildren will direct other people to the One who served them by giving His life (Matthew 20:28).

- our grandchildren develop humility, allowing them not only to serve but also to be served (John 13:5).

Lord, you emptied yourself of all that was rightly yours so you could come to serve us. We are so grateful for your sacrifice, humility, and love. I thank you for the younger generation. They are eager to serve. Their desire to serve comes from having a "first love" attitude toward you. May their example challenge us as adults to do better and to be more generous. May they keep the flame of service burning brightly as they stay close to you. Thank you for the Christian leaders who mentor our young people. Give them strength and wisdom. Help us to rekindle our love for you and to renew our commitment to serve. Amen.

Think and Do

- Read Max Lucado's *The Crippled Lamb* with younger grandchildren. Allow them to discuss their feelings about the story and to express empathy for the little lamb.

- If "example is leadership" (Albert Schweitzer), what is your involvement in meeting the needs of the hurting people in your community and around the world? How is your example leading your grandchildren to serve others?

- Find the missionary stories of Gladys Aylward (1902–1970), Mary Slessor (1848–1915), Hudson Taylor (1832–1905), and/or Jim Elliot (1927–1956) to share with your older grandchildren. Each of these missionary heroes exemplifies loving service.

- Spend some time researching organizations that provide compassionate ministries to children, and enlist the entire family to support a child or take part in a feeding project.

"Let each of you look out not only for his own interests, but also for the interests of others" (Philippians 2:4 NKJV).

"My brothers and sisters, believers in our glorious Lord Jesus Christ must not show favoritism" (James 2:1).

"Command them to do good, to be rich in good deeds, and to be generous and willing to share" (1 Timothy 6:18).

"Serve wholeheartedly, as if you were serving the Lord, not people, because you know that the Lord will reward each one for whatever good they do, whether they are slave or free" (Ephesians 6:7–8).

"Do nothing out of selfish ambition or vain conceit. Rather, in humility value others above yourselves" (Philippians 2:3).

day six:
THE WAY HOME

Love, not anger, brought Jesus to the cross. Golgotha came as a result of God's great desire to forgive.

Richard Foster

May I never boast except in the cross of our Lord Jesus Christ.

Galatians 6:14

In Max Lucado's book *And the Angels Were Silent,* the author recounts the wonderful story of Charing Cross.

Charing Cross is one of the most recognized landmarks in London. It is near the geographical center of the city and serves as a navigational tool for those confused by the streets. A little girl was lost in the great city. A policeman found her. Between sobs and tears, she explained she didn't know her way home. He asked her if she knew her address. She didn't. He asked her phone number; she didn't know that either. But when he asked her what she knew, suddenly her face lit up. "I know the Cross," she said. "Show me the Cross and I can find my way home from there."[4]

Isn't this the earnest prayer of every Christian grandparent? Don't we pray that our grandchildren will always be able to find their way safely home?

Three times a year, our church has a Family Gathering. On these Sundays we celebrate what God has done through the ministry of our church. We also honor God's work in the lives of individuals and families.

Baptisms are the highlight of the service. During one of these celebrations, it was touching to watch the baptism of nine-year-old Zachary. People being baptized are invited to choose someone to be involved in this important step on their spiritual journey. They can choose to be baptized by a pastor, a family member, a teacher, or a friend who has inspired them spiritually.

That Sunday, Zach walked toward the baptistery with an older man. Zach had chosen his grandpa.

Zach's mom explained to me that when she asked him why he had chosen his grandfather, her son's answer was simple and direct. "Because when we visit him, Grandpa always talks about God."

Zach's parents encouraged and nurtured his faith. His church loved and supported him. And his faithful grandfather had been a crucial part of the process, lovingly helping Zachary find his way home.

The cross is central to our beliefs. It was on the cross that Jesus gave His physical life to purchase eternal life for us. The cross is precious.

As grandparents, we pray that our grandchildren will understand the meaning of the cross. May they each turn to the cross of Christ and find their way home.

Let Us Pray That . . .

- our grandchildren look to the cross of Christ for forgiveness (Colossians 1:13–14).

- our grandchildren understand that their sins have been nailed to the cross and experience the freedom that comes with that knowledge (Colossians 2:14).

- our grandchildren fix their eyes on things above, not on earthly things (Colossians 3:2).

- our grandchildren experience peace and reconciliation with God through the cross of Christ (Colossians 1:19–20).

- our grandchildren cling to the cross until it guides them home (Galatians 6:14).
- our grandchildren feel honored to tell others about what Christ has done for them on the cross (Mark 16:15).

Father, in the cross of Christ we glory. Without Christ's sacrifice on the cross we would be totally helpless and hopeless. Thank you for the cross and for the salvation provided there. Father, I pray that my grandchildren will grasp the significance of the cross. I pray that they will love the Savior who died there on their behalf. When they are feeling lost, fearful, and alone, may they look to the cross and find their way home. Amen.

Think and Do

- Take some time to reflect on the cross and its significance in your life. Read Galatians 6:14. Do you boast in the cross of Christ?
- When did you first turn to the cross? Do your grandchildren know that story?
- Plan to read Max Lucado's book *The Christmas Child* with your grandchildren during the next Christmas season. Talk about the importance of this Little One, who would some-day go to the cross for them.
- Give your grandchild a unique cross necklace for a special occasion.

"For he has rescued us from the dominion of darkness and brought us into the kingdom of the Son he loves, in whom we have redemption, the forgiveness of sins" (Colossians 1:13–14).

"Having canceled the charge of our legal indebtedness, which stood against us and condemned us; he has taken it away, nailing it to the cross" (Colossians 2:14).

"Fixing our eyes on Jesus, the pioneer and perfecter of faith. For the joy set before him he endured the cross, scorning its shame, and sat down at the right hand of the throne of God" (Hebrews 12:2).

"God was pleased to have all his fullness dwell in him, and through him to reconcile to himself all things, whether things on earth or things in heaven, by making peace through his blood, shed on the cross" (Colossians 1:19–20).

"May I never boast except in the cross of our Lord Jesus Christ, through which the world has been crucified to me, and I to the world" (Galatians 6:14).

"Go into all the world and preach the gospel to all creation" (Mark 16:15).

day seven:
BLESSINGS

Prayers go up and blessings come down.
Yiddish Proverb

Out of his fullness we have all received grace in place of grace already given.

John 1:16

Holding babes in arms and dragging older children by the hand, parents pushed through the crowds, eager to get to Jesus. Mark 10 tells us these parents were on a mission. They were bringing their children to Jesus to be blessed.

For years, I have wondered exactly what each one wanted. What did they think the Lord's blessing on their child would bring? Did they want Jesus to speak words of kindness to their little one?

In a culture unfriendly to children, did they hope his touch would bring healing or guarantee a trouble-free future? Would community leaders recognize their child as extraordinary because Jesus had blessed him or her?

I suppose the parents all had their own hopes and longings as they brought their beloved child to Jesus. Yet I imagine their desires were similar to what mine would have been for my child or grandchild.

I would have wanted Jesus to gather my grandchild into His arms so she could experience firsthand His love and care. I would have wanted her to look into Jesus' eyes and carry forever the memory of His kindness and compassion.

These are the things I pray for today.

We often pray that God would bless our children and grandchildren. Frequently, our prayers are for very specific blessings of God. Many years ago, I learned a strategy for prayer from the Lighthouse Movement. This method has stayed with me, and I continue to use it to pray for my children and grandchildren.

Using the acronym BLESS, this simple approach reminds us to pray for detailed needs in the lives of those we love.

B—Body. We can pray for physical needs and protection.

L—Labor. We can pray for daily activities, whether at work or school.

E—Emotions. We can pray for emotional health, strength, and maturity.

S—Social. We can pray for relationships with friends, family, co-workers, and teachers.

S—Spiritual. We can pray for a growing and thriving relationship with Christ.

Let's follow this acronym and begin today with the letter B. Let us pray for God's blessings for our grandchildren's physical needs of health and safety.

Let Us Pray That . . .

- our grandchildren experience health and long life (Psalm 91:16).

- our grandchildren receive protection and physical safety through their relationship with God (Psalm 4:8).

- our grandchildren, understanding that they are fearfully and wonderfully made by God, make peace with their physical attributes and develop a healthy body image (Psalm 139:13–16).

- our grandchildren treat their bodies with the respect and care that honors God (1 Corinthians 6:19–20).

- God protects our grandchildren from harmful substances and helps them comprehend the consequences of addictions (1 Peter 5:8).

- our grandchildren understand that even in times of physical suffering, nothing can separate us from the love of Christ (Romans 8:38–39).

Giver of Life, thank you for the precious gift of life. We praise you that our grandchildren were fearfully and wonderfully made. I pray for their health. Please protect them at home, school, work, and play. May they learn to appreciate life and understand that they are your unique creation. Father, may they resist the temptation to engage in risky and dangerous behavior that would cause them great harm. Help us to model self-care and good habits. Protect them from people who would hurt them or involve them in activities that would cause irreparable harm. May they live long, healthy, and productive lives that honor and glorify you. Amen.

Think and Do

- Read Psalm 139. Many young people struggle with their body image because of faulty messages in the media. How does this psalm challenge the negative messages kids confront daily? What encouragement can you give your grandchildren about their physical attributes?

- Max Lucado's book *You Are Special* reminds children (and adults) that God loves them just the way they are. Use this book to begin a discussion with your grandchildren about their true value.

- How do you model self-care to your grandchildren? Do they see you going for walks? Getting enough rest? Taking vacations? Are there any small changes you need to make in your daily routines that would honor God, give you a better quality of life, and offer a positive example to your grandchildren?

"He will call on me, and I will answer him; I will be with him in trouble, I will deliver him and honor him. With long life I will satisfy him and show him my salvation" (Psalm 91:15–16).

"In peace I will lie down and sleep, for you alone, LORD, make me dwell in safety" (Psalm 4:8).

"For you created my inmost being; you knit me together in my mother's womb. I praise you because I am fearfully and wonderfully made; your works are wonderful, I know that full well" (Psalm 139:13–14).

"Do you not know that your bodies are temples of the Holy Spirit, who is in you, whom you have received from God? You are not your own; you were bought at a price. Therefore honor God with your bodies" (1 Corinthians 6:19–20).

"For I am convinced that neither death nor life, neither angels nor demons, neither the present nor the future, nor any powers, neither height nor depth, nor anything else in all creation, will be able to separate us from the love of God that is in Christ Jesus our Lord" (Romans 8:38–39).

day eight:
A CHILD'S WORK

Laziness may appear attractive, but work gives satisfaction.

Anne Frank

For we are God's handiwork, created in Christ Jesus to do good works, which God prepared in advance for us to do.

Ephesians 2:10

Author Bruce Winston uses this humorous story in his work with leaders:

For many days, an old farmer had been plowing with an ox and mule together, and working them pretty hard. The ox said to the mule, "Let's play sick today and rest a little while." The old mule said, "No, we need to get the work done, for the season is short." But the ox played sick, and the farmer brought him fresh hay and corn and made him comfortable. When the mule came in from plowing, the ox asked how he had made out. The mule said, "We didn't get as much done, but we made it all right, I guess."

The ox asked, "What did the old man say about me?" "Nothing," said the mule.

The next day the ox, thinking he had a good thing going, played sick again.

When the mule came in very tired again, the ox asked, "How did it go?" "All right, I guess, though we didn't get much done."

The ox also asked, "What did the old man say about me?" "Nothing to me," was the reply, "but he stopped and had a long talk with the butcher."

Oftentimes in life, when we refuse to work, bad things can happen![5]

The L in our acronym BLESS encourages us to pray for our grandchildren's work, or *labor*. An important task of childhood is learning to take initiative and work hard. Life can be even harder than necessary for adults who have not learned that bad things can happen when we refuse to work hard.

Unfortunately, adults often assume that learning these critical life skills comes easily to children. It doesn't.

Getting on the yellow bus for the first time, learning to spell and read at the kitchen table, taking standardized tests, or clocking in for their first job are great accomplishments for our grandchildren. Each new skill requires a ton of work and emotional stamina.

Many children experience crippling fear, anxiety, and discouragement as they embark on these adventures. Some become afraid of failure, and they retreat. These children need our support and our prayers. They need our encouragement to persevere and be diligent. The degree to which they develop initiative and diligence can determine their level of satisfaction with adult life.

Play is an important part of developing a good attitude toward work. In the words of noted play therapist Gary Landreth, "Play is a child's 'work,' and the 'toys' are his words." Playing with our grandchildren not only creates emotional bonds but also helps children gain focus and attention. Children need free time to imagine and play. Children with rich playtimes develop into creative and confident adults.

When we pray for our grandchildren's school activities, projects, tests, playtime, sports, music lessons, and other concerns, we are entering their world. We are expressing love and concern in a manner they can feel and appreciate. Let us pray today for our grandchildren, big or small, as they engage in their work, whatever that may be.

Let Us Pray That . . .

- our grandchildren's work and learning environment includes kind, caring, and patient individuals who deal with them tenderly (Isaiah 40:11).

41

- our grandchildren's temperament and learning styles are accepted and encouraged, not condemned (Romans 15:7).
- any learning difficulties are recognized and addressed.
- our grandchildren retain what they are learning and have some measure of satisfaction in their work (Proverbs 22:29).
- our grandchildren learn to handle school difficulties with grace and resiliency (Jeremiah 29:11).
- our grandchildren have great memories of rich and imaginative playtimes.
- our grandchildren enter adulthood motivated to work hard, to be responsible, and to do the good works prepared in advance for them to do (Ephesians 2:10).
- our grandchildren honor God with their strengths, talents, abilities, and spiritual gifts (Colossians 3:17).

Heavenly Father, you created us to gain satisfaction from our work. I pray that each of my grandchildren discovers his or her own unique set of gifts and abilities and enters a profession that brings satisfaction. May each fulfill his or her God-given potential. Today as my grandchildren learn and grow, I pray that they be surrounded by kind and caring Christian mentors who not only encourage them but also hold them accountable. Give me the grace to applaud each success, to encourage each glimpse of diligence, and to do whatever I can to help them gain a healthy perspective on work. I pray, Lord, that as they face discouragement in school or at work, they develop the resiliency that comes from trusting you. Thank you, Lord, for these unique individuals. May they embrace your call on their lives. Amen.

Think and Do

- How do you approach work? How do you handle work frustrations? When was the last time your family members heard you talk about the positive aspects of your work?
- How can you create an environment for your visiting grandchildren that encourages lifelong learning? Choosing books

wisely, planning activities that involve creative play, going for walks, or taking trips to the zoo or aquarium can whet a child's appetite to know more about the world.

- Do you know your grandchildren's interests, strengths, and talents? Take the time this week to ask questions and to get to know your grandchild so you can affirm his strengths. Help him picture a bright future using his God-given gifts. Pray with your grandchild about his future.

"He tends his flock like a shepherd: He gathers the lambs in his arms and carries them close to his heart; he gently leads those that have young" (Isaiah 40:11).

"Accept one another, then, just as Christ accepted you, in order to bring praise to God" (Romans 15:7).

"Do you see someone skilled in their work? They will serve before kings; they will not serve before officials of low rank" (Proverbs 22:29).

" 'For I know the plans I have for you,' declares the LORD, 'plans to prosper you and not to harm you, plans to give you hope and a future' " (Jeremiah 29:11).

"We urge you, brothers and sisters, warn those who are idle and disruptive, encourage the disheartened, help the weak, be patient with everyone" (1 Thessalonians 5:14).

"For we are God's handiwork, created in Christ Jesus to do good works, which God prepared in advance for us to do" (Ephesians 2:10).

"And whatever you do, whether in word or deed, do it all in the name of the Lord Jesus, giving thanks to God the Father through him" (Colossians 3:17).

day nine:
EMOTIONALLY HEALTHY KIDS

If you want your children to improve, let them overhear the nice things you say about them to others.

Haim Ginott

A person finds joy in giving an apt reply—and how good is a timely word!

Proverbs 15:23

Billy Graham frequently shared this story.

A man and his wife visited an orphanage where they hoped to adopt a child. In an interview with the boy they wanted, they told him in glowing terms about the many things they could offer him. To this he replied, "If you have nothing to offer except a good home, clothes, toys, and the other things that most kids have, why, I would just as soon stay here."

"What on earth could you want besides those things?" the woman asked. "I just want someone to love me," replied the boy.[6]

I can guarantee that what every child most wants is the love of his family—including the love of his grandparents. "The grandparent/child relationship is second only to the parent/child connection in a child's emotional growth," says Susan Bosak, author of *How to Build the Grandma Connection*.[7]

Feeling parental (and grandparental) love and acceptance is critical to every child's emotional and spiritual development.

Kids flourish in the unconditional love of the entire family. The E in our acronym BLESS encourages us to pray for our grand-children's *emotions*.

Being secure in their attachment to Mom, Dad, Grandma, and Grandpa enables children to cope with the frustrations and dis-appointments of life. Unconditional love establishes an unshak-able, safe platform from which they may take flight and enjoy the adventure of life. Most important, children who experience the unwavering affection and acceptance of family can easily move forward in a trusting and loving relationship with God.

There is a significant movement in the church today. It is a revolution that is challenging Christians to grow in emotional health. Peter Scazzero, author of *The Emotionally Healthy Church*, was in the throes of midlife and experiencing wrenching relational and emotional pain before he grasped a vital truth.

The church planter/pastor reached this life-changing conclu-sion: "Emotional health and spiritual maturity are inseparable."[8] It is true. Children who are struggling emotionally may love the Lord and want to serve Him, but they are on shaky ground spiritually as they try to comprehend the concept of God's unconditional love.

Wouldn't it be better to establish the foundation for emotional and spiritual health early in life? Someone has said, "It is easier to build up a child with our words than it is to repair an adult."

For children and adolescents, emotional health and spiritual maturity are rooted in the unconditional love and acceptance of parents and grandparents. All children struggle emotionally as they move through various developmental stages. But we can help by showing unconditional love.

Pastor Andy Stanley says that when children are deprived of unconditional love, they become exasperated (Ephesians 6:4). I have seen this exasperation. Sometimes, it looks like anger. Other times, it looks like rebellion. Frequently, it looks like de-pression or underachievement. Some go to extreme measures to cope with the grief and loss.

Pastor Stanley is correct. However a child responds, the ex-asperation is often the result of the child being uncertain of the love and commitment of the parents.

Unconditional love is what our grandchildren want and need most from us.

We can pray that our grandchildren will be certain of our love and commitment to them. We can ask the Lord to help us as we point them to Jesus, the One who loves them best.

Let Us Pray That . . .

- our grandchildren feel secure in the love of their parents and grandparents (Ephesians 6:4).
- our grandchildren feel our affection.
- our grandchildren have tender memories of their childhood.
- our grandchildren experience grace and empathy from their family members (Ephesians 4:32).
- our grandchildren receive honestly affirming words and actions from their families (Ephesians 4:29).
- our grandchildren feel the support and prayers of family during the hard times of life (Philippians 4:6).
- the adults in our grandchildren's lives do not shrink back from providing discipline (Proverbs 3:12).
- our grandchildren adopt healthy, compassionate, and realistic ways of thinking about themselves and others (Philippians 4:8).
- our grandchildren learn to manage anger and other strong emotions in a constructive way (Ephesians 4:26).

Father, we praise you because you are love. You have shown us the extent of your unconditional love by sending your one and only Son to the cross for us. No words can express our gratitude for your infinite love and sacrifice. I pray, Lord, that my grandchildren will accept your unconditional love and will grow in the grace and knowledge of Jesus. I thank you that you have created us to be emotional beings. I thank you for the gifts of laughter and of tears. May my grandchildren find the freedom to express their emotions with me because they are confident of my love. Teach me how to sincerely love and encourage them. May I daily model the unconditional love you offer to us. Help me to remember to always point them to your love. Amen.

Think and Do

- Child development expert Haim Ginott said, "If you want your children to improve, let them overhear the nice things you say about them to others." What kind things can you say about your grandchildren in front of friends and family?
- Everyone loves to hear stories of when they were little. What stories can you tell your grandchildren of the days when they were very young?
- *Mind Coach* by Dr. Daniel Amen can help children correct faulty assumptions they have about themselves and life. Read this book with your grandkids and help identify any faulty thinking they might have.

"Fathers, do not exasperate your children; instead, bring them up in the training and instruction of the Lord" (Ephesians 6:4).

"Be kind and compassionate to one another, forgiving each other, just as in Christ God forgave you" (Ephesians 4:32).

"Do not let any unwholesome talk come out of your mouths, but only what is helpful for building others up according to their needs, that it may benefit those who listen" (Ephesians 4:29).

"Do not be anxious about anything, but in every situation, by prayer and petition, with thanksgiving, present your requests to God" (Philippians 4:6).

"The LORD disciplines those he loves, as a father the son he delights in" (Proverbs 3:12).

"Finally, brothers and sisters, whatever is true, whatever is noble, whatever is right, whatever is pure, whatever is lovely, whatever is admirable—if anything is excellent or praiseworthy—think about such things" (Philippians 4:8).

" 'In your anger do not sin': Do not let the sun go down while you are still angry" (Ephesians 4:26).

day ten:
A CIRCLE OF FRIENDS

Is any pleasure on earth as great as a circle of Christian friends by a good fire?

C. S. Lewis

A friend loves at all times.
Proverbs 17:17

A faculty meeting at Merton College in March of 1926 was the starting point for a remarkable friendship between C. S. Lewis and J. R. R. Tolkien. The professors shared a love for literature and a passion for writing. As the friendship developed and trust grew, Tolkien and Lewis would sit with colleagues at a local pub, discussing their latest writing projects. Lewis, cherishing a lifelong love for fairy tales, listened intently as his new friend shared stories of Middle Earth.

Tolkien's unwavering faith was the topic of many conversations with Lewis, an equally determined atheist. Having suffered great loss as a child, Lewis doubted the existence of a personal and loving God.

Friends for nearly five years, Tolkien and Lewis engaged in a life-changing late-night conversation in September of 1931. Soon after, Lewis converted to Christianity and embarked on a spiritual journey that has touched millions of lives.

Tolkien profoundly affected Lewis' life in every way. Not only did Lewis become a devout Christian, but his writing and use of fantasy also became a venue for communicating his faith.

The wonderful world of Narnia came to life. Intertwining the truth of Christianity with this enchanting and beautiful world, Lewis wrote stories that continue to charm and awaken readers spiritually today.

If C. S. Lewis had not had the support and encouragement of J. R. R. Tolkien, the world may never have experienced the literary genius of this great Christian writer and philosopher. And to think it all began with a routine faculty meeting at Merton College!

Our grandchildren's friendships are of great consequence. They can either spur our grandchildren on to become everything God meant them to be or they can put up barriers to their spiritual, emotional, or relational growth. Our grandchildren's friendships can lead them to develop their God-given gifts in a healthy way or set them on a path toward a tragic detour.

Experts in child development believe that children adopt the values of the people who they feel love them most. Our children definitely need loving, supportive friends—but loving, supportive friends with strong moral values.

Friends can bring our grandchildren great joy, encouragement, and challenge. Friends can also drain, discourage, and sadden. As grandparents, we can pray for life-giving friendships for our grandchildren.

Today, as we pray for the first S in our BLESS acronym, let's ask God to strengthen our grandchildren's *social* lives by giving them healthy, moral, loving friendships.

Let Us Pray That . . .

- our grandchildren avoid relationships with angry people (Proverbs 22:24).

- our grandchildren avoid morally negative relationships (1 Corinthians 15:33).

- our grandchildren are blessed with caring and loyal friends for a lifetime (Proverbs 17:17).

- our grandchildren feel loved and secure in their family and listen to friendship advice from parents and grandparents (Proverbs 1:8).

- our grandchildren see Jesus Christ as their dearest friend (John 15:15).
- we are loving and nonjudgmental toward their friends, and at the same time willing to provide gentle guidance (Ephesians 4:2).

Dearest Friend, I rejoice in the fact that you call us your friends. I thank you for all that the word friend *means. You have chosen us for the intimacy of friendship. Lord, I ask that my grandchildren will understand they can have a friendship with you. I pray that you would bring kind and moral people into their lives. May their friends encourage them to do what is right and to follow you. May my grandchildren learn how to be good friends to their peers. May they support their friends in times of trouble, pray for them, and always point them to Jesus. Give them discernment in choosing friends, and may their friendships help them to become the people you want them to be. Forgive me when I criticize their friendships. May our home be a place where healthy relationships can flourish. Amen.*

Think and Do

- Who was your best friend during your elementary school years? High school? College? Do you have any funny stories to tell? Do you have any stories of the strength this relationship gave you? Do you have any stories of caution? Share these stories and any pictures you may have of these friends.
- Read 1 Samuel 18:1. This verse describes the most famous friendship in Scripture. How would you describe this friendship from this single verse? What do you hope your grandchildren will find in their friendships?
- *My Friend Jesus* by Kathryn Slattery tells the gospel story in a kid-friendly way. This would be a wonderful addition to your library for your preschool and early elementary-aged grandchildren.

"Do not make friends with a hot-tempered person, do not associate with one easily angered, or you may learn their ways and get yourself ensnared" (Proverbs 22:24–25).

"Do not be misled: 'Bad company corrupts good character' " (1 Corinthians 15:33).

"A friend loves at all times, and a brother is born for a time of adversity" (Proverbs 17:17).

"Listen, my son, to your father's instruction and do not forsake your mother's teaching" (Proverbs 1:8).

"Instead, I have called you friends, for everything that I learned from my Father I have made known to you" (John 15:15).

"Be completely humble and gentle; be patient, bearing with one another in love" (Ephesians 4:2).

day eleven:
LET THE CHILDREN COME

Every child you encounter is a divine appointment.

Wes Stafford

I have been reminded of your sincere faith, which first lived in your grandmother Lois and in your mother Eunice and, I am persuaded, now lives in you also.

2 Timothy 1:5

Raised by a determined atheistic father and a sometimes atheist, sometimes Episcopalian mother, renowned author Anne Lamott believed in God on the sly. Despite being forced by her father to sign a pact committing to a life of atheism, Anne reports that she "backslid" into faith at an early age. "Even when I was a child," she says, "I knew that when I said 'Hello,' someone heard."

My conviction that children can enjoy a relationship with God is unshakable. How many of us cherish our own personal stories of a close relationship with God during our childhood? A boy or girl's innocence, sincerity, spontaneity, and trust make him or her perfect candidates for friendship with God.

For many years I treasured a worn and folded sheet of lined school paper that I kept in my wallet. When discouraged or sad, I would take it out, smooth out the wrinkles, and read the moving words printed on the paper by our second daughter, Julie, at the age of seven, and forever imprinted on my heart: *God, I will always love you.*

Samantha, my granddaughter, is preoccupied with the outdoors. She relishes every minute spent with the trees, flowers, grass, sky, and many bugs, which she counts as friends. Recently, the promise of taking a walk brought on a serious case of the wiggles. Getting her out the door was a challenge. Who knew that putting on sandals could be such an ordeal?

Mid-wiggle, she paused long enough to lift one foot high. She admired it for just a moment and then smiled at me. When I asked her who had made her toes, she enthusiastically replied, "Jesus made my toes!"

Our grandson Kevin is fascinated with the lives of missionaries. At the age of twelve, our kind, sincere, and intelligent grandson is wondering what God has in mind for his future.

Yes, children can enjoy a relationship with God. Jesus applauded their humble nature. Calling a young child to stand before the disciples, Jesus reminded His friends that there was much they could learn from a child: "Therefore, whoever takes the lowly position of this child is the greatest in the kingdom of heaven" (Matthew 18:4).

Jesus loves children and invites them into a relationship with him: "Let the little children come to me" (Mark 10:14).

The last S in our BLESS acronym reminds us to pray for our grandchildren's *spiritual* lives.

Let Us Pray That . . .

- we as Christian parents, grandparents, teachers, and pastors will have the same loving, inviting attitude toward our grandchildren that Jesus did (Mark 10:14).

- we as Christian parents, grandparents, teachers, and pastors take seriously Jesus' teaching about children (Matthew 18:10).

- no one stands in the way or creates roadblocks to our grandchildren's faith (Matthew 18:6).

- our grandchildren recognize the God of creation and worship Him (Psalm 19:1).

- our grandchildren move toward a warm and loving relationship with Jesus during childhood (Mark 10:14).

- our grandchildren will sense the presence of God in their lives (Psalm 102:28).

- each of our grandchildren has a vibrant faith in Christ (Galatians 3:26).

- our grandchildren will keep their childlike faith all of their lives (Matthew 18:3–4).

Loving Father, thank you for being present in the lives of small children. May we learn to trust you with the simplicity and love that comes so easily to them. I pray that my grandchildren will experience your presence and know you are always there for them. I ask that no one will ever put any roadblocks in their path that will hinder them from knowing your love and grace. May the Christian adults in their lives be free of hypocrisy and demonstrate the love and acceptance of your Son. May we welcome children the way Jesus did. Amen.

Think and Do

- Read Wes Stafford's book *Too Small to Ignore* and discuss with other grandparents the importance of children in the life of the church. What can our age group do to elevate the church's ministry to children? Is there a children's ministry project at your church to which you could give your time or finances or prayers?

- Take some time to reflect on your own childhood. Can you recall specific times when you were aware of God's presence or care? Where can you see the fingerprints of God in your childhood? How can this help you understand what might be going on in the internal spiritual lives of your grandkids?

- Write down a couple of stories from your early relationship with God. Someday you may want to share these stories with your family.

"When Jesus saw this, he was indignant. He said to them, 'Let the little children come to me, and do not hinder them, for the kingdom of God belongs to such as these' " (Mark 10:14).

"See that you do not despise one of these little ones. For I tell you that their angels in heaven always see the face of my Father in heaven" (Matthew 18:10).

"If anyone causes one of these little ones—those who believe in me—to stumble, it would be better for them to have a large millstone hung around their neck and to be drowned in the depths of the sea" (Matthew 18:6).

"The heavens declare the glory of God; the skies proclaim the work of his hands. Day after day they pour forth speech; night after night they reveal knowledge" (Psalm 19:1–2).

"The children of your servants will live in your presence; their descendants will be established before you" (Psalm 102:28).

"So in Christ Jesus you are all children of God through faith" (Galatians 3:26).

"Truly I tell you, unless you change and become like little children, you will never enter the kingdom of heaven. Therefore, whoever takes the lowly position of this child is the greatest in the kingdom of heaven" (Matthew 18:3–4).

day twelve:
EVERYDAY CHRISTIANS

Wherever you are—be all there.

Jim Elliot

And whatever you do, whether in word or deed, do it all in the name of the Lord Jesus, giving thanks to God the Father through him.

Colossians 3:17

Hunched over her gray Formica table, with Webster's dictionary open before her, my grandmother labored over the crossword puzzle in the local newspaper. The silence was broken by the shrill whistle of a copper teakettle. I poured the bubbling water into two green jadeite mugs and began to brew our tea.

A crossword puzzle, saltine crackers, and Red Rose tea with a teaspoon of sugar were part of my grandmother's afternoon routine. Sitting across from her at the little table, I sipped the steaming hot tea as she pushed aside the worn dictionary in favor of a story about her brother Robert who died of influenza or about her childhood friend Betsy with the long, chestnut curls.

Lazy afternoons at Grandmother's house seemed endless, and tea never tasted as good as when sipped from those old green mugs.

In the dining room, Grandmother's buffet held exquisite serving dishes, sparkling pink goblets, and delicate teacups. Fascinated by each piece, I imagined her smoothing the crocheted lace tablecloth and setting the table with her fine china in preparation for a party or fancy dinner.

Yet, if I could return to my grandmother's home and carry away a memento of my days with her, I would not retrieve one of her finer things. Instead, I would lay claim to those precious green jadeite mugs.

I love everyday, common, useful, available things—things we connect with the comings and goings of life. I value things that sometimes require a little repair or a little scouring to remove a stain, yet are the things I can depend on to be there.

Most of my life, however, I've wanted to be one of the "finer things" like the elegant teacups in Grandma's dining room. I've wanted to look just right, be admired, unique, and brought out for special occasions.

I've wasted too much time pursuing that.

The hours spent at my grandma's kitchen table taught me a valuable lesson. This lesson is one that I want my grandchildren to embrace:

I want to be an Everyday Christian—worn, comfortable, and continually used. I want God to open the kitchen cupboard and use me in any way that opens people's hearts, bringing moments of comfort and joy and hope.

Being an Everyday Christian will inevitably lead to some sin stains that will require scouring, and bumps and chips from life that will require repair. I can accept that. I desire to play a part, no matter how small, in the daily, ordinary lives of fellow believers.

The New Testament is filled with examples of everyday Christianity. Jesus elevated the simple act of giving a cup of cold water in His name or washing the feet of another believer as an act of love. Paul commands us to forgive each other for the daily bumps and bruises of life, to offer hospitality, to encourage and pray for one another.

Common stuff was sacred to Jesus. Daily life was filled with opportunities to serve on the most basic of levels.

For many years, our daughter-in-law Lindy has cared for developmentally disabled adults. Each year, the residents in the home where she works are taken on a short vacation by a staff member. On one of these outings, Lindy spent an afternoon and evening in our home with one of her residents, a young man who neither talks nor walks and is completely dependent on the care of others.

Our daughter-in-law fed him, dressed him, encouraged him, loved him, and laughed with him. I watched as she entered his everyday world with kindness and patience and treated him with dignity and respect.

Lindy is an Everyday Christian.

Grandma extended love by sharing cups of tea and life stories at her worn table. We too can give love and hope in ordinary ways as we prepare a meal, hold a hand, listen to others, make a bed, do laundry, calm fears, dry a tear, or read God's Word in answer to someone's need.

My definition of an *Everyday Christian* is this: "Someone who offers Jesus in the sacred, everyday moments of life."

Just as I treasured the everyday things in my grandmother's house, I believe God treasures and rejoices over His followers who give no thought to recognition or admiration, but who eagerly seek opportunities to serve Him and others.

I pray that my grandchildren will become Everyday Christians who share hope and love with a hurting world.

Let Us Pray That . . .

- our grandchildren will be protected from the desire for greatness (Luke 9:46).
- our grandchildren will not seek glory for themselves but for Jesus (John 3:30).
- our grandchildren understand that greatness comes from serving (Luke 22:26).
- our grandchildren will be clothed with humility (Colossians 3:12).
- our grandchildren learn to offer words of hope to everyone (1 Peter 3:15).

Gracious Father, so many Everyday Christians have crossed my path. Thank you for the sincerity and simplicity of their service.

Give me the heart of an Everyday Christian. I pray that my grandchildren will focus on loving you and loving other people more than on accomplishments and recognition. May they experience the greatness that comes from serving you. I pray that they will relish the everyday experiences of life and see you in the common things. May they be grateful for every moment you give to them. And may they use these moments to share hope and love with others. May my grandchildren become Everyday Christians. Amen.

Think and Do

- What are some everyday opportunities you have to serve? Are you ever tempted to see the everyday tasks of life as unimportant?
- Have you met some Everyday Christians? What are some of the characteristics of those who live out their faith every day?
- What temptations to greatness do Christians struggle with today?
- Reflect on John 3:30. What would it mean for Christ to increase and you to decrease?
- What ministry could you become involved in to model this level of servanthood to your grandchildren?

"An argument started among the disciples as to which of them would be the greatest. Jesus, knowing their thoughts, took a little child and had him stand beside him. Then he said to them, 'Whoever welcomes this little child in my name welcomes me; and whoever welcomes me welcomes the one who sent me. For it is the one who is least among you all who is the greatest' " (Luke 9:46–48).

"He must become greater; I must become less" (John 3:30).

"Instead, the greatest among you should be like the youngest, and the one who rules like the one who serves" (Luke 22:26).

"Therefore, as God's chosen people, holy and dearly loved, clothe yourselves with compassion, kindness, humility, gentleness and patience" (Colossians 3:12).

"But in your hearts set apart Christ as Lord. Always be prepared to give an answer to everyone who asks you to give the reason for the hope that you have" (1 Peter 3:15).

day thirteen:
THE NAMES OF GOD

What we believe about God is the most important thing about us.

A. W. Tozer

Our Father in heaven, hallowed be your name.

Matthew 6:9

Names are important. We carefully chose each of our children's names.

The name Jennifer brought to my mind an active little girl full of life and excitement. So when our first child was born, we named her Jenny. It was the perfect choice. She truly is intelligent, curious, and full of life. She has brought much excitement and joy to our family. Her shiny, copper-colored hair earned her the nickname Jenny the Penny, given by her grandfather.

Because of some scary moments before he was born, we named our son Jonathan—God's gracious gift. With his sense of humor and generous spirit, that is exactly what he has been to every member of our family.

One of my dearest friends, Julie, was a kind and gentle mother. When our third child was born, I couldn't imagine anything we could want more than for this little girl to have that same gentle, loving spirit. Julie is now a gentle, loving mother herself.

When our last child was born, we were out of J's. Big sister Jenny chose the name for our last little girl. She named her Joy. From her first day with our family, she has brought us great joy.

Everyone who meets her says the same thing: "The name Joy suits her perfectly."

Names are precious.

There is no name more important than that of our heavenly Father. Not only is He holy but His very name is also holy.

You can find many passages of Scripture that speak about the importance of revering God's name. Exodus 20:7 warns us against misusing God's name. Philippians 2:10 tells us that someday every knee will bow at the sound of that beautiful name.

For thousands of years, believers have found comfort in God's name, and millions have cried out His name in moments of peril. All of us have come before God's throne in Jesus' name. We love the name of God.

There is nothing more important to our grandchildren's well-being than that they understand who God is and show reverence and respect for their heavenly Father's name.

We are often careless when speaking the name of God. Some people are more than careless. Their use of God's name borders on disrespect, and it is frightening to think of the consequences of this disregard for His name.

My prayer is that my grandchildren will understand the holy nature of God and the holiness of His name. I pray that they will only utter His name with reverence and affection. May they call it out in times of trouble, find comfort in His name in moments of sorrow, and boldly come to His throne in the name of Jesus.

Let Us Pray That . . .

- our grandchildren acknowledge the holiness of God (Luke 1:49).
- our grandchildren always speak His name with reverence and love (Psalm 115:1).
- our grandchildren understand the power of the name of God (Matthew 18:20).
- our grandchildren proclaim His holiness to others and worship Him (Psalm 29:2).

- our grandchildren have an accurate theology based on the truth of God's Word (2 Timothy 2:15).

- our grandchildren wholeheartedly believe the Scriptures that teach us about the nature of God (2 Timothy 3:16).

- our grandchildren love the name of God (Psalm 5:11).

Holy and Almighty One, I adore you for your holiness and perfection. I thank you for revealing your holiness to us through your Word and through creation. Lord, I am so finite and your holiness so infinite, yet I ask that you would give me a greater understanding of your holiness. I pray that my grandchildren will recognize your holiness. I ask that you would work in their hearts till they have such reverence for you and your name that they would always speak your name with respect and care. May they search your Word to learn more about who you are. May they bow before you with awe. May they come to know you as . . .

Almighty	Light of the World
Ancient of Days	Lover of our Souls
Beautiful One	Majestic
Comforter	Mighty One
Creator	Merciful
Delight	Never-changing
Deliverer	Omnipotent, Omnipresent, Omniscient
Eternal One	Powerful
Everlasting Father	Prince of Peace
Faithful One	Quietness
Forgiver	Redeemer
Friend	Refuge
Good	Rest
Gracious	Salvation
Healer of Broken Hearts	Shepherd
Hiding Place	Song

Holy	Strength
Humble	Triumphant
Infinite	Truth
Judge	Unfailing
Kind	Victorious
King	Wonderful Counselor
Lamb of God	Worthy of All Praise

Think and Do

- Read Psalm 62:1–2. What do these verses tell you about the nature of the God we serve? Are other passages especially meaningful to you as you think of the attributes of God?

- Choose two or three of the attributes of God from the prayer above. Can you think of a time when God has shown that attribute to you? Write a paragraph or two about God's work in your life relevant to those attributes. Save these to share with your grandchildren.

- You may want to purchase a copy of *God's Names* by Sally Michael. It is a beautiful book and can be a springboard for gentle, meaningful bedtime conversations when the grandkids spend the night. Knowing the names of God can provide our grandchildren with the security and hope they will need all of their lives.

"You are enthroned as the Holy One; you are the one Israel praises" (Psalm 22:3).

"Not to us, LORD, not to us but to your name be the glory, because of your love and faithfulness" (Psalm 115:1).

"For where two or three gather in my name, there am I with them" (Matthew 18:20).

"Ascribe to the LORD, you heavenly beings, ascribe to the LORD glory and strength. Ascribe to the LORD the glory due his name; worship the LORD in the splendor of his holiness" (Psalm 29:1–2).

"Do your best to present yourself to God as one approved, a workman who does not need to be ashamed and who correctly handles the word of truth" (2 Timothy 2:15).

"All Scripture is God-breathed and is useful for teaching, rebuking, correcting and training in righteousness, so that the servant of God may be thoroughly equipped for every good work" (2 Timothy 3:16–17).

"But let all who take refuge in you be glad; let them ever sing for joy. Spread your protection over them, that those who love your name may rejoice in you" (Psalm 5:11).

day fourteen:
ON THE JOB SITE

God is God. Because He is God, He is worthy of my trust and obedience. I will find rest nowhere but in His holy will.

Elisabeth Elliot

Your will be done, on earth as it is in heaven.

Matthew 6:10

Tyler's grandfather managed a construction company. The five-year-old would often call his grandparents' home early in the morning, hoping to talk to his grandfather before he hopped in his truck and headed to the work site.

One morning, before Grandma had a chance to yawn a sleepy, "Good morning," Tyler blurted out, "I need to talk to Grandpa. I want to know if I can go to the job site with him today."

His grandmother, my wise friend Jan, later reflected on her grandson's sincere request and made an important observation. "I wonder if our heavenly Father waits for us to begin our days by asking if we can go to the job site with Him."

In many ways, Tyler's desire to work alongside his grandfather offers insight into this portion of the Lord's Prayer: "Your will be done on earth as it is in heaven." God invites us to join Him in carrying out His will in the world.

Tyler wanted to accompany his grandfather to the work site because he loved him. The loving relationship we share with our heavenly Father motivates us to do our utmost to do His will in the world.

Perhaps there is a secret to doing God's will on earth as it is done in heaven. Could our finest obedience, our most earnest and complete obedience, occur only when our hearts overflow with love for Him?

Does our obedience best display the activity of heaven when we understand the privilege and honor bestowed on us as we work together with God and do His will in all things?

Does it thrill the heart of God when we seek to do His will with all of our heart—when we ask Him if we can go with Him to the work site?

Our grandchildren will need to mature in obedience in the same way we are still pressing forward daily to maturity. I hope my grandchildren will begin many a day asking their heavenly Father for the opportunity to join Him in His work in the world.

Let Us Pray That . . .

- our grandchildren will have a growing desire to understand and do God's will (Romans 12:2).

- our grandchildren acknowledge God in all their decisions and choices and allow Him to direct their paths (Proverbs 3:5–6).

- our grandchildren understand that God has a good and perfect plan for them that they can trust without reservation (Jeremiah 29:11).

- our grandchildren humbly seek guidance and counsel for important decisions (Proverbs 19:20).

- our grandchildren reject the temptation to do God's will out of a legalistic attitude, but rather obey God because of fully devoted hearts (Psalm 86:11).

- our grandchildren learn, as we are learning, to obey God daily from willing and loving hearts (Matthew 6:10).

Sovereign Lord, you are the Creator and Ruler of the universe. You are continually at work in our world. There is no greater privilege than to serve you. Thank you for inviting us to be part of your mission on Earth. Forgive me for the thousands of times I have chosen my will and ignored yours. I pray that my grandchildren will have a growing desire to do your will. May they obey your will in their daily lives and seek to align themselves with your work in the world. Amen.

Think and Do

- Read and meditate on Psalm 112:1: "Blessed are those who fear the LORD, who find great delight in his commands." What blessings come to those who delight in God's will?

- Do you recall a time when you obeyed God and it was pure delight? Did your obedience stem from a legalistic attitude toward the will of God, or was there another motivation behind your obedience?

- *The Lord's Prayer* by Rick Warren is filled with beautiful illustrations your grandchild will find inspirational and encouraging. Reading this with your grandchildren will create a heartwarming memory and allow you to address the important issue of God's will.

"Do not conform to the pattern of this world, but be transformed by the renewing of your mind. Then you will be able to test and approve what God's will is—his good, pleasing and perfect will" (Romans 12:2).

"Trust in the LORD with all of your heart and lean not on your own understanding; in all your ways submit to him, and he will make your paths straight" (Proverbs 3:5–6).

" 'For I know the plans I have for you,' declares the LORD, 'plans to prosper you and not to harm you, plans to give you hope and a future' " (Jeremiah 29:11).

"Listen to advice and accept discipline, and at the end you will be counted among the wise" (Proverbs 19:20).

"Teach me your way, LORD, that I may rely on your faithfulness; give me an undivided heart, that I may fear your name" (Psalm 86:11).

"Your will be done, on earth as it is in heaven" (Matthew 6:10).

day fifteen:
DAILY BREAD

God created us to have needs, not counting them as sinful or selfish. Without them, we'd have no way of knowing our need for God or how much He loves us.

Anonymous

Therefore I tell you, do not worry about your life, what you will eat or drink; or about your body, what you will wear. Is not life more than food, and the body more than clothes? Look at the birds of the air; they do not sow or reap or store away in barns, and yet your heavenly Father feeds them. Are you not much more valuable than they?

Matthew 6:25–26

Monsieur Mahault endured the German occupation of Paris during World War II. As a very young boy, he suffered loss, fear, and physical hunger during this horrific time. These many years later, his stories were haunting for him and heartrending to us.

As we shared *un café* at his dining room table, he chronicled the years when the most basic food items were scarce. It was normal for his family to go days without even a slice of bread.

Even after sixty years, he fought back tears upon entering a French bakery. The ability to buy freshly baked bread and even to smell its aroma filled him with gratitude.

Bread. It symbolizes our most basic needs.

Jesus invites us to come to Him with everyday needs. "Give us today our daily bread" (Matthew 6:11). His words were not only an invitation but also a declaration that everything we would ever need to nourish body or soul would come from Him.

Jesus calls us to absolute dependence on Him. In these simple words, He invited us to see His generosity and goodness in what He provides for us each day. Jesus is our living Bread of Life. He is the bread that satisfies our physical, emotional, and spiritual hungers, and we can count on Him in all circumstances.

In a world dominated by self-sufficiency, materialism, and greed, our grandchildren can confidently turn to Jesus for their everyday needs and then in turn share what He gives with those who are hurting.

Let Us Pray That . . .

- our grandchildren recognize God as the source of all things and are sincerely grateful for every good gift God gives them (Psalm 145:15–16).

- our grandchildren bring their needs to their heavenly Father (Philippians 4:19).

- our grandchildren will be content with having their daily needs met (Proverbs 30:8).

- our grandchildren eventually will be able to differentiate between a want and a need (Philippians 4:12).

- our grandchildren open their hands to offer help to those in need (Proverbs 31:20).

Jehovah Jireh, you provided a sacrificial lamb for Abraham. You provided the Sacrificial Lamb to atone for our sins. How can we ever doubt that you will provide for us? Thank you for your provision of our daily bread. May my grandchildren trust you each day for their needs. Teach them to be content with what you provide. I pray today for the millions who are without bread in this world because of oppression and famine. Meet their needs, O Lord, we pray. Help us to always remember that Jesus is the Living Bread. Amen.

Think and Do

- Recall a time when God specifically answered a prayer for your needs. How can you share this story with your grandchildren?
- When praying at mealtimes, take advantage of this opportunity to model gratitude for the way God meets your daily needs.
- Ask your grandchildren to name things God provides for them. Start with "A" and name something that begins with each subsequent letter of the alphabet. "Thank you, God, for apples. Thank you, God, for books." Be sure to take your turn.
- Do you bake bread? Have your grandchildren help you make a loaf of bread for a special dinner. As you mix and knead, you can mention the Lord's Prayer and Jesus' instructions that we pray for our daily bread.

"The eyes of all look to you, and you give them their food at the proper time. You open your hand and satisfy the desires of every living thing" (Psalm 145:15–16).

"My God will meet all your needs according to the riches of his glory in Christ Jesus" (Philippians 4:19).

"Keep falsehood and lies far from me; give me neither poverty nor riches, but give me only my daily bread" (Proverbs 30:8).

"I know what it is to be in need, and I know what it is to have plenty. I have learned the secret of being content in any and every situation, whether well fed or hungry, whether living in plenty or in want. I can do all this through him who gives me strength" (Philippians 4:12–13).

"She opens her arms to the poor and extends her hands to the needy" (Proverbs 31:20).

day sixteen:
COMPLETE FORGIVENESS

No child of God sins to that degree as to make himself incapable
of forgiveness.

John Bunyan

And forgive us our debts . . .
Matthew 6:12

Imagine the care with which Moses outlined to the Hebrew
people the specific instructions for celebrating the Passover
meal. I presume the head of the household had the responsibility to not only slaughter the lamb but also to sweat over hot
coals to roast it. And it was undoubtedly the patriarch who had
the sober task of painting the blood of this spotless sacrificial
lamb on the doorframes of the family home.

When the preparations were complete, the family gathered
around the table in quietness and sadness to share this solemn
meal. Jewish moms and dads, grandmas and grandpas, boys
and girls had all witnessed God's deliverance with the previous
nine plagues. Surely they had no doubt that this tenth plague
would become a sad reality. Some of those who would lose
their lives that night might have been playmates or neighbors. In
the midst of these sober moments, they were also anticipating
the promised exodus from Egypt the following day.

At midnight, heartbreaking screams and pitiful sounds
of mourning filled the country as the angel of death moved
through the streets of the city, striking down the firstborn in

every Egyptian home. The grief and loss was inescapable and devastating to the Egyptian people.

However, the Israelites had nothing to fear from this angel of death. As the angel approached a Jewish home, he did not stop for a moment to consider who was inside, how many people were there, what their occupations might have been, or even what commandments they may have broken. The angel's attention was riveted to the doorframes where the blood of the lamb had been placed. As soon as he saw the blood, he "passed over" the home. Because, "All that matters is the blood."

When I heard Erwin Lutzer speak the phrase above in a Good Friday message years ago, my life changed. For so long, I assumed that my sins were so grave and so disappointing to God that they were only slightly forgiven. In spite of sincere confession, residual guilt and condemnation continued to plague me.

Suddenly, I grasped that no sin (including my own) is more powerful than the blood of Christ. No mistake, error, weakness, flaw, or sin can stand up to the love of God for us expressed in the cross of Christ.

To believe our sin is greater than God's ability to forgive borders on arrogance. Hebrews 7:25 has become a comfort. "Therefore he is able to save completely those who come to God through him, because he always lives to intercede for them."

Jesus lived and died to bring us complete, freedom-giving, peace-producing, joy-filling, heavenly forgiveness that restores us to intimacy with our heavenly Father.

In the Lord's Prayer, Jesus invites us to come to Him and ask for the forgiveness He so longs to give. I pray that my grandchildren will run to Jesus to experience the total, peace-giving forgiveness paid for at the cross.

Let Us Pray That . . .

- our grandchildren understand that confession and repentance are vitally important to forgiveness (Acts 3:19; 1 John 1:9).

- our grandchildren learn the important phrase, "I am sorry" (James 5:16; Matthew 7:3–5).

- our grandchildren regularly examine their lives (1 Corinthians 11:28).

- our grandchildren understand that God loves them dearly and forgives freely (Ephesians 1:7; Romans 3:24).
- our grandchildren understand that God washes away all of their sins until they are as white as snow (Isaiah 1:18).
- our grandchildren understand that God has removed their sins as far as the east is from the west (Psalm 103:12).
- our grandchildren realize they are free from condemnation (Romans 8:1).
- our grandchildren will be joyful over the gift of forgiveness that has been given to them (Ephesians 2:8).

Forgiving Father, Jesus, our high priest, meets our needs by being holy, blameless, and pure. He is exalted above the heavens. I am so grateful for the complete forgiveness He has provided for me. I pray that my grandchildren will understand and accept the complete forgiveness purchased for them at the cross. May they not spend their lives weighed down by guilt and condemnation, but rather live with freedom and joy. I pray that they will share this good news of forgiveness with others so they too can know what it is like to be free from condemnation. May this complete forgiveness energize them to live worthy of their calling in Christ Jesus. Amen.

Think and Do

- How forgiven are you? Ten percent forgiven? Forty percent forgiven? Seventy-five percent forgiven? Or one hundred percent forgiven? What would change in your life if you lived as a one-hundred-percent forgiven and reconciled believer? How would this benefit your family?
- Psalm 51:7 and Isaiah 1:18 both promise that the Lord will wash us and make us whiter than snow. When was the last time you felt that clean? Is there something keeping you from experiencing the complete forgiveness of Christ?
- Spend some time reviewing Isaiah 43:25 and 44:22. Which concept would you most like to communicate to your

grandchild? Can you think of a creative way to communicate this truth about forgiveness?

"Repent, then, and turn to God, so that your sins may be wiped out, that times of refreshing may come from the Lord" (Acts 3:19).

"If we confess our sins, he is faithful and just and will forgive us our sins and purify us from all unrighteousness" (1 John 1:9).

"Therefore confess your sins to each other and pray for each other so that you may be healed. The prayer of a righteous person is powerful and effective" (James 5:16)

"Why do you look at the speck of sawdust in your brother's eye and pay no attention to the plank in your own eye? How can you say to your brother, 'Let me take the speck out of your eye,' when all the time there is a plank in your own eye? You hypocrite, first take the plank out of your own eye, and then you will see clearly to remove the speck from your brother's eye" (Matthew 7:3–5).

"Everyone ought to examine themselves before they eat of the bread and drink from the cup" (1 Corinthians 11:28).

" 'Come now, let us settle the matter,' says the LORD. 'Though your sins are like scarlet, they shall be as white as snow; though they are as red as crimson, they shall be like wool" (Isaiah 1:18).

"As far as the east is from the west, so far has he removed our transgressions from us" (Psalm 103:12).

"Therefore, there is now no condemnation for those who are in Christ Jesus" (Romans 8:1).

"For it is by grace you have been saved, through faith—and this is not from yourselves, it is the gift of God—not by works, so that no one can boast" (Ephesians 2:8–9).

day seventeen:
A FORGIVING HEART

No prayers can be heard which do not come from a forgiving heart.

J. C. Ryle

. . . as we also have forgiven our debtors.

Matthew 6:12

It was a peaceful October morning in Lancaster County, Pennsylvania. At 9:51 a.m., peace and tranquility were the furthest things from the heart and mind of Charles Carl Roberts IV. This troubled man charged into an Amish schoolhouse intent on shattering the peace of the Lancaster community. Charles Roberts shot and killed ten little girls and then ended his own life.

Families around the world condemned the senseless violence and joined the grieving families in mourning their inconceivable loss. The compassion and dignity of the bereaved families astounded journalists.

Nothing impressed the world more than the immediate demonstrations of grace and forgiveness by the devastated families toward the perpetrator's family. Even before the funeral, members of the Amish community visited the home of Roberts' widow and mourning children, determined to express love and to comfort the Roberts family in their own grief and loss.

How were they able to do this? How could they so readily forgive someone who had inflicted such pain?

This Amish community has fashioned a culture of forgiveness. Their beliefs come directly from the Gospels. They have embraced the words of Jesus that Christians are to forgive in the same way that they have been forgiven.

In a society that emphasizes personal rights, payback, and revenge, forgiveness is a hard concept to grasp, much less to put into action.

What would happen if Christians took seriously Jesus' call to forgive? What could change in our churches if we were to push grudges aside and reach out in grace to those who have hurt us? How would our families benefit if tenderness and compassion were more often our first response to unkindness or anger?

Nothing is more critical to the spiritual and relational well-being of our grandchildren than following the biblical lessons on forgiveness.

Let Us Pray That . . .

- our grandchildren grow in their understanding of the forgiveness they have been given (Matthew 18:21–30).

- our grandchildren's hearts soften toward anyone who has hurt them (Ephesians 4:32).

- our grandchildren do not hold grudges (Colossians 3:13).

- our grandchildren will have a healthy and balanced understanding of forgiveness toward others (1 Thessalonians 5:14).

- our grandchildren will be at the forefront of creating a culture of biblical forgiveness.

- our grandchildren will realize that choosing the path of forgiveness is difficult and that they need God's help in order to forgive as Christ has forgiven (Romans 8:26).

Father, I confess my own hard and unforgiving heart. I pray that you will soften my heart so I can truly pray, "Forgive us our debts as we have forgiven our debtors." May my church become a church that models biblical forgiveness. I pray that my grandchildren will have hearts that are always ready to forgive. May they resist the temptation to hold grudges and be known as people who easily forgive. Give them the strength to forgive when it is difficult. May they understand that they have been given mercy so they can give mercy to others. Amen.

Think and Do

- Robert Frost wrote of "two roads" that "diverged in a yellow wood." He chose the road "less traveled by," and this choice "made all the difference." Could it be that forgiveness is "the [road] less traveled by" in the Christian life? What steps do you need to take to get on the path to a life of forgiveness toward others? What choices do you need to make? Do you need spiritual guidance and support in this area?

- What difference would a forgiving heart make in your daily life? Who would you be without the bitterness or hard feelings you harbor against another? To whom do you need to offer the gift of forgiveness?

- For younger children, *The Coat of Many Colors* by Jenny Koralek teaches important lessons on love and forgiveness. Older children may enjoy *Shiloh*, the story of a boy and a beagle. This dramatic story by Phyllis Reynolds Naylor will help middle schoolers with issues of kindness and forgiveness.

"Then Peter came to Jesus and asked, 'Lord, how many times shall I forgive my brother or sister who sins against me? Up to seven times?' Jesus answered, 'I tell you, not seven times, but seventy-seven times' " (Matthew 18:21–22).

"Be kind and compassionate to one another, forgiving each other, just as in Christ God forgave you" (Ephesians 4:32).

"Bear with each other and forgive one another if any of you has a grievance against someone. Forgive as the Lord forgave you" (Colossians 3:13).

"Make sure that nobody pays back wrong for wrong, but always strive to do what is good for each other and for everyone else" (1 Thessalonians 5:15).

"Let us then approach God's throne of grace with confidence, so that we may receive mercy and find grace to help us in our time of need" (Hebrews 4:16).

day eighteen:
LEAD US

Lead us, heavenly Father, lead us, o'er the world's tempestuous sea;
guard us, guide us, keep us, feed us, for we have no help but Thee.

James Edmeston

He guides me along the right paths for his name's sake.

Psalm 23:3

For weeks, Mrs. Taylor reminded our fourth-grade class that we would soon receive a visit from the Gideon Bible man. Once a year during each of my six years at Stark Elementary School, the jovial, white-haired man arrived with his cardboard box of Bibles; black, brown, white, and sometimes red. He was eager to reward one of the precious Bibles to anyone who would tackle a long list of memory verses.

Each grade received an age-appropriate list to memorize. As he talked to us about the importance of reading the Bible, I was captivated. Perhaps it was because of the kindness in his voice or maybe it was his passion for the Bible. For whatever reason, after his presentation I struggled to concentrate on math or social studies. My mind kept returning to the thin sheet of paper with a list of verses, tucked away in my desk.

Sitting at the worn wooden desk as the afternoon sun peeked through the green shades, I made a decision. Each verse was a treasure, and I would faithfully memorize and claim these treasures as my own.

I do not recall which year we memorized Psalm 23. I do remember receiving a small New Testament with Psalms for memorizing the psalm along with other key Scriptures. I also remember how I loved David's words. Each line painted a picture, and the arrangement of each phrase was music to my ears.

I imagined a loving shepherd stroking tired lambs. Wooly lambs curled up very near to one another in long, thick, cool, green grass, the kind of grass you love to run through with bare feet. Other times, the shepherd coaxed them to a quiet stream for a drink of cool water. Of course, the shepherd led his flock down safe paths. Well known for going on ahead of his sheep, the shepherd scouted out the best route. Sometimes the way was steep or difficult, but the shepherd kept a close eye on his sheep and knew exactly what they could handle. He always escorted them to safety.

According to the psalmist, the shepherd guides his sheep in "paths of righteousness for His name's sake" (v. 3 NKJV). As long as the sheep kept their eyes on the shepherd, following the path he walked before them, they would be secure.

In the prayer that Jesus taught, He instructs us to pray, "Lead us not into temptation, but deliver us from the evil one" (Matthew 6:13). Over the years, I struggled with the meaning of these words. As I reflect as well on Psalm 23, I now picture within the Lord's Prayer the Shepherd leading His flock. He would never lead them astray.

Is this portion of the Lord's Prayer a prayer for our moral and spiritual safety?

Theologian J. I. Packer, in his work on the Lord's Prayer, suggests that these two phrases, "Lead us not into temptation" and "deliver us from the evil one," are a plea that God would rescue us from crushing temptations and trials.

Packer concludes his discussion on this portion of the Lord's Prayer by wondering if these words, "Lead us not into temptation, but deliver us from evil," are simply a cry from the depths of our hearts, "Father, keep us safe."

I pray that my grandchildren will loyally follow the Shepherd, who will lead them wisely down the right path. In addition, when faced with overwhelming temptation and trials, I cry out on their behalf, "Father, keep them safe."

Let Us Pray That . . .

- our grandchildren understand that they have a Shepherd who offers to gently lead them (Psalm 100:3).
- our grandchildren recognize the moral safety that comes from following the path set out for them by God (Psalm 16:11).
- our grandchildren will be like Daniel in avoiding temptation (Daniel 1:8).
- our grandchildren look to God for help when temptations and difficulties are overwhelming (1 Corinthians 10:13).
- our grandchildren listen for the Shepherd's voice and follow only Him (John 10:27).
- our heavenly Father keeps our grandchildren morally and spiritually safe (Matthew 6:13).

Gracious Shepherd, thank you for being a kind and caring Shepherd. Forgive me for the times I have strayed like a stubborn sheep down paths that lead me into moral danger. It is my desire to follow your paths of righteousness. Father, I pray for my grandchildren. I pray that they will be captivated by the thought of you as the kind and gentle Shepherd of their souls. May they commit themselves to following you closely, trusting that you will lead them to green pastures and still waters. Lord, when we consider all of the dangers and temptations that are so prevalent in our world today, we cry out to you on behalf of our grandchildren. Father, keep them safe. Amen.

Think and Do

- *A Child's Look at the 23rd Psalm* by W. Phillip Keller is an important children's classic. This book was written after Keller's bestseller, *A Shepherd Looks at Psalm 23*. This book, first printed more than thirty years ago, can still be enriching for adult believers.

- What wisdom can you share with your grandkids about following the Shepherd? Was there a time in your childhood when you decided to follow your own path, instead of following the Shepherd? What were the consequences? Is it a story you can share discreetly with your grandchildren? What short and compassionate admonitions can you give about intentionally avoiding moral temptations?

- Depending on where you live, you may be able to find a sheep farm that would allow your family to make a short visit. A tour by the owner could give your grandchildren valuable insight into the difficulties the shepherd faces in caring for the sheep.

"Know that the LORD is God. It is he who made us, and we are his; we are his people, the sheep of his pasture" (Psalm 100:3).

"You make known to me the path of life; you will fill me with joy in your presence, with eternal pleasures at your right hand" (Psalm 16:11).

"But Daniel resolved not to defile himself with the royal food and wine, and he asked the chief official for permission not to defile himself this way" (Daniel 1:8).

"Flee from sexual immorality" (1 Corinthians 6:18).

"Submit yourselves, then, to God. Resist the devil, and he will flee from you" (James 4:7).

"No temptation has overtaken you except what is common to mankind. And God is faithful; he will not let you be tempted beyond what you can bear. But when you are tempted, he will also provide a way out so that you can endure it" (1 Corinthians 10:13).

"My sheep listen to my voice; I know them, and they follow me" (John 10:27).

"And lead us not into temptation, but deliver us from the evil one" (Matthew 6:13).

day nineteen:
GLORY

The glory of God is a human being fully alive; and to be alive consists in beholding God.

St. Irenaeus

So whether you eat or drink or whatever you do, do it all for the glory of God.

1 Corinthians 10:31

Two broad-shouldered men carted Frère Joseph up the steps and into the foyer of the tiny French church. Once inside, they carefully set the elderly gentleman back on his feet, and he immediately shuffled to his usual chair near the back of the sanctuary. Crippled by arthritis, he struggled to climb stairs or walk long distances without assistance. Still, the ninety-year-old maintained a mental and spiritual strength and determination that defied his age.

Frère Joseph was by no means frail. A steady handshake from his calloused hands hinted at his former strength and told tales of a lifetime of hard work.

However, having lost most of his sight and much of his hearing, Frère Joseph found living on his own no longer possible. Despite the physical challenges brought on by aging, he was unwavering in his desire to attend the church he had loved for more than fifteen years—even if it meant he had to be carried.

As other worshipers arrived and dashed to their places, they took a moment to greet him with a kiss on each cheek and a loving "Bonjour, Frère Joseph!"

The service began with my husband reading from God's Word. Daniel, a caring friend to Frère Joseph, realized that the older man expected someone to open his Bible to the passage. He scurried to his side to flip the pages. Before the faithful page-turner could locate chapter and verse, Frère Joseph spoke aloud the very same words my husband was reading. Spending a lifetime studying God's Word meant he knew these words by heart.

French Protestant churches frequently celebrate the Lord's Supper with a common cup. In total silence, the loaf of bread and cup of wine passed down the rows from person to person. The cup reached Frère Joseph. I knew exactly what to expect.

With arthritic hands, the longtime follower of Christ grasped the cup, lifted it above his head, and whispered, "To God be the glory."

I have rarely experienced as worshipful a moment as when our elderly friend raised the cup and his heart to God in praise. Years later, as I sit in our quiet sanctuary preparing to take communion, I frequently find myself lifting the communion cup and whispering those same words: "To God be the glory."

As we age, it becomes more challenging to maintain an attitude of praise. We can falsely believe our days of being used by God are over and done. Our focus may shift from glorifying God to lamenting our own problems and struggles.

In the midst of such painful moments, it would help us to open our Bibles to Psalm 92. Whether we are nine or ninety, the goal of our lives remains the same.

We are all here to glorify God.

My grandchildren will not always be young. I would like to model graceful aging for them. I also pray that they will glorify God every day of their lives.

Let Us Pray That . . .

- our lives, notwithstanding our age or challenges, clearly bring glory to God (Psalm 34:1).

- as we age, we reject self-pity and isolation in favor of a growing faith and devotion (Psalm 92:1).
- our grandchildren mature in the understanding that the goal of their lives is to glorify God in all they do and for all of their years (Psalm 89:1).
- our churches initiate occasions for intergenerational experiences where our grandchildren can see God at work in people of all ages (Leviticus 19:32).

Heavenly Father, we will extol you all the days of our lives. You are worthy to receive glory and honor. I am so grateful to have known believers who have glorified you even when life was difficult. Lord, I pray that my grandchildren will have hearts that desire to glorify you. When faced with difficult circumstances, may they have the resolve to praise you at all times. May they have the joy of knowing older believers who are filled with contentment and peace. May our hearts join as one in saying, "To God be the glory." Amen.

Think and Do

- Read Psalm 92. What concepts are helpful to you as you think about serving God all your days? Are there areas— physical, emotional, mental, financial, or spiritual—where you need support and encouragement in order to maintain a grateful, praiseful attitude?
- Psalm 92:14–15 promises that we can produce spiritual fruit at any age. The psalmist declared, "The LORD is upright; he is my Rock." List at least fifteen ways God has been your Rock throughout your life. Find natural opportunities to proclaim God's faithfulness to the next generation.
- The next time you participate in communion, remember the words of Frère Joseph: "To God be the glory."

"I will extol the LORD at all times; his praise will always be on my lips" (Psalm 34:1).

"It is good to praise the Lord and make music to your name, O Most High, proclaiming your love in the morning and your faithfulness at night" (Psalm 92:1–2).

"I will sing of the Lord's great love forever; with my mouth I will make your faithfulness known through all generations" (Psalm 89:1).

"Stand up in the presence of the aged, show respect for the elderly and revere your God. I am the Lord" (Leviticus 19:32).

day twenty:
JESUS SHAKES THINGS UP

We are to be spiritually poor only for the sake of becoming spiritually rich, detached from what we can own so that we can be attached in a different way to what we cannot own, detached from consuming so that we can be consumed by God.

Peter Kreeft

Blessed are the poor in spirit, for theirs is the kingdom of heaven.

Matthew 5:3

"I just need to shake things up a bit."

I have heard those words in my office. Sometimes it means the person is bored with life and is considering going skydiving. If the person is the more cautious type, he or she might need some courage to choose chicken salad for lunch rather than a burger.

At other times, people who say this are bored with their spouse and want to pick a fight, or worse. If it is a healthier situation, they may have made an appointment in hopes of learning skills that will change the ineffective ways of relating that are killing the relationship.

Sometimes people want to "shake things up" through political dissent or demonstrations, hoping to call attention to their cause.

Sometimes we "shake things up" by doing something that to others is totally unexpected or out of character for us: changing jobs, learning to fly an airplane, booking tickets for a long-dreamed-of-vacation, starting lessons to play a musical instrument, moving to another state.

I recall serving roast beef for Christmas dinner instead of turkey, and that is a "shake up" my family still remembers. I may not do that again for a while.

But "shake ups" are often good for us.

The greatest "shake up" in history came through Jesus. For the Jewish establishment, the Sermon on the Mount was a "shake up" of monumental proportions. I can imagine bearded Pharisees gathering their robes, puffing their cheeks in disgust, and turning away as Jesus taught the eager crowds these foreign concepts. "He is crazy!" must have been their haughty response to the first of His utterances as they marched away, leaving clouds of dust behind them.

"Blessed are the poor in spirit, for theirs is the kingdom of God."

The Jewish leaders were the last group that would ever acknowledge they were spiritually impoverished. They were banking on their own good works, observance of the Law, and superiority over the common person. Jesus' words were a slap to their complacency and pride.

Most commentators view Jesus' words in the same way. Jesus spoke of a poverty that results in blessing. When we are "poor in spirit," we admit our emptiness before God. We are in no position to accept all the riches He has to offer until we are thoroughly aware of our need.

Normally, I wouldn't pray that my grandchildren would be poor. This is an exception. I pray that my grandchildren will see their own spiritual bankruptcy and turn to Jesus for all their spiritual needs.

I am grateful for the "shake up" Jesus brought in so many ways to our understanding of spirituality. The greatest "shake up" of all came at the cross.

In dying, He gave us life.

Let Us Pray That . . .

- our grandchildren will recognize their emptiness and their need and turn to God (Psalm 40:17).

- our grandchildren will be humble and understand that their own efforts will never meet their spiritual need (Psalm 18:27; Isaiah 64:6).
- our grandchildren find their satisfaction in life from their relationship with Christ (Psalm 63:3).
- our grandchildren will be eternally rich (Ephesians 2:6–7).
- we model humility and dependence upon God for our righteousness (2 Timothy 4:8).

Lord, you have shaken my religious beliefs to the core. The only way I can receive the riches you offer is by humbly acknowledging my own poverty. This is hard to accept. Help me to see how spiritually poor I am. I pray that early in the lives of my grandchildren, they will become aware of their own spiritual poverty and need for you. May they have the humility and faith that leads them to totally depend on you. I pray they will find spiritual riches in Jesus. Amen.

Think and Do

- Where do the teachings of Jesus "shake up" your understanding of life and spirituality? Are you in need of a "shake up" right now?
- Read Luke 18:9–14 and notice the spiritual pride of the Pharisee. Contrast that attitude with the humility of the tax collector. How is it possible for Christians to succumb to spiritual pride today? How can you set an example of trusting in the mercy of God?

"I am poor and needy; may the Lord think of me. You are my help and deliverer; you are my God, do not delay" (Psalm 40:17).

"You save the humble but bring low those whose eyes are haughty" (Psalm 18:27).

"All of us have become like one who is unclean, and all our righteous acts are like filthy rags" (Isaiah 64:6).

"Because your love is better than life, my lips will glorify you. I will praise you as long as I live, and in your name I will lift up my hands. I will be fully satisfied as with the richest of foods; with singing lips my mouth will praise you" (Psalm 63:3–5).

"And God raised us up with Christ and seated us with him in the heavenly realms in Christ Jesus, in order that in the coming ages he might show the incomparable riches of his grace, expressed in his kindness to us in Christ Jesus" (Ephesians 2:6–7).

"Now there is in store for me the crown of righteousness, which the Lord, the righteous Judge, will award to me on that day—and not only to me, but also to all who have longed for his appearing" (2 Timothy 4:8).

day twenty-one:
COMFORT

Earth has no sorrow that heaven cannot heal.
"Come, Ye Disconsolate"

Blessed are those who mourn, for they will be comforted.
Matthew 5:4

I did not catch the names of the authors. I don't even remember the title of the book. Yet there was information shared in the radio interview I shall never forget.

While doing research for their book on family life, the husband and wife writing team questioned dozens of adults about loss during their childhood years. Specifically, the authors asked each person to describe a time during childhood when someone had tenderly comforted them. Only one-third of those responding could recall a time when they had been comforted by an adult. Sadly, most had simply muddled through disappointing and difficult life circumstances alone.

It is heartbreaking to think that so many of us have traveled through life without experiencing tender comfort for our pain—heartbreaking and true.

Loss and disappointment, mourning and grief. In life, these are inevitable. Children lose pets, friends, favorite toys, and sometimes grandparents. Parents accept job transfers and children frequently move away from the only home they have known and the familiar surroundings that are secure. Divorce disrupts family life, school life, and normal routines, and children feel shaky. Childhood losses matter.

Children mourn as surely as adults do. Many children enter adult life with unresolved loss and pain.

When I was seven, my grandfather died suddenly of a heart attack. Our family was in shock. It seemed that no one comprehended the grief and loss experienced by the children in the family. We were comfortless. Without any adult comforters, it took us many years to recover from the loss of this central figure in our childhood.

We cannot bring back the friends, pets, security, or people our grandchildren have lost. We cannot put an end to their pain. But we can offer words of comfort, understanding, and kindness. We can model healthy mourning. Even small children can absorb lessons on how to comfort others in the future by experiencing comfort themselves.

Comforting our grandchildren in times of need reminds them that they are not alone. Our presence can strengthen them and help them get through hard times.

My prayer is that when asked, my adult grandchildren will be able to point to times in their childhood when our family offered them the comfort and support they needed. I pray they will each have a friend who will provide them with comfort and encouragement at just the right moment.

Even more important, I pray that they will discover "the God of all comfort" (2 Corinthians 1:3), who will attend to their mourning and bring them genuine, enduring peace and comfort.

Let Us Pray That . . .

- we will have wisdom and use the right words to provide comfort, reassurance, and healing to our grandchildren in times of need (Proverbs 16:24).

- we will have wisdom for the times when our grandchildren do not need our words, but rather need us to sit quietly with them in their pain.

- we will be sensitive to the losses and grief of childhood and not minimize our grandchildren's concerns (Romans 12:15).

- our grandchildren find the God of all comfort (2 Corinthians 1:3).
- our grandchildren learn to comfort family members and friends during loss and disappointment (2 Corinthians 1:4).

Father of All Comfort, your constant care is a source of comfort to us. When I remember that you have cared for our family in the past, I know that you will care for us today. Lord, I pray that my grandchildren will turn to you for comfort in the difficulties of life. May they always be aware of your reassuring presence. Help us to embrace our grandchildren with our love and support in times of need and be a source of comfort to them. May we all hold tightly to the eternal comfort that comes only from you. Amen.

Think and Do

- What was your greatest loss during childhood? Who was your comforter at that time? What did you learn from that person? If you did not have a comforter, what do you wish someone would have done to help you through that time?

- Do you know the greatest losses experienced by your grandchildren? Listen to your grandchildren's everyday conversations and stories and note any underlying losses: relationships, reputation, comfort, favorite toys, pets, or activities.

- When we feel pity, we feel sorry for and lament someone else's pain. When we comfort, we offer meaningful physical touch and words of reassurance that give strength and hope. The next time a family member suffers loss, offer both sympathy and comfort.

"Gracious words are a honeycomb, sweet to the soul and healing to the bones" (Proverbs 16:24).

"Rejoice with those who rejoice; mourn with those who mourn" (Romans 12:15).

"Praise be to the God and Father of our Lord Jesus Christ, the Father of compassion and the God of all comfort, who comforts us in all our troubles, so that we can comfort those in any trouble with the comfort we ourselves receive from God. For just as we share abundantly in the sufferings of Christ, so also our comfort abounds through Christ" (2 Corinthians 1:3–5).

day twenty-two:
AN OBSESSION WITH SMALLNESS

Meekness is the most untranslatable of words.

William Barclay

Do not think of yourself more highly than you ought, but rather think of yourself with sober judgment, in accordance with the faith God has distributed to each of you.

Romans 12:3

The New Testament word for *meekness* is challenging to translate into English. It is even more challenging to put into practice. Our culture's notion of meekness varies from gentleness and kindness to weakness and passivity, and it falls far short of the biblical meaning.

Biblical scholars explain that the meekness Jesus extolled in the Sermon on the Mount was a rare kind of humility and gentleness. As I meditate on the Gospels, I have come to realize that the life of Jesus was the flawless picture of this uncommon and powerful humility, and that I personally fall short of this gentleness and humility by many miles.

In *The Gospel According to Tolkien*, author Ralph Wood suggests that Tolkien's lovable hobbit characters embody biblical meekness. Wood believes that Tolkien created his characters as small in stature precisely to challenge our "obsession with largeness."

He explains that the hobbits were not only small in size but also had zero ambition for greatness. The merry little people of the Shire delighted in giving gifts to others on their own birthdays. These hobbits were astonishingly free of lust for power and control, and they relished the love and affection, loyalty and faithfulness of their fellow hobbits. Their faithfulness to one another and their aversion to ambition were the exact qualities that made them central and powerful figures in the destruction of the evil that ravaged Middle Earth. Wood remarked, "For the hobbits, bigger does not mean better, and small can indeed be beautiful." [9]

A hunger for greatness, power, control, or superiority is the antithesis of meekness. A yearning to love and serve behind the scenes for the benefit of others may be the finest description of biblical meekness.

Meekness is countercultural. We suffer from an "obsession with largeness." Our society screams at our grandchildren that fame, fortune, power, and greatness determine an individual's worth and value.

Admittedly, humility in our grandchildren's relationship with God, considering the welfare of others, serving with no desire for recognition, being teachable, and exercising patience, self-control, and trust when wrongly accused will not get them very far in this world.

If they choose the difficult path of following the example of Jesus, they will eventually discover that there is great strength in surrendering an "obsession with largeness" for an investment in gentleness, humility, sacrifice, and service.

I know what an ongoing struggle this will be. But I pray that they will pursue meekness and humility, because these qualities will draw them closer to Jesus and bring blessings of another, more lasting kind.

Let Us Pray That . . .

- we learn to be humble and gentle like Jesus (Matthew 11:29).
- our grandchildren will have an accurate view of themselves, grounded in Scripture (Romans 12:3).

- our grandchildren will not have the false humility that comes from a low self-concept but rather will understand that they are precious to God (Psalm 139:17–18).
- our grandchildren understand meekness not as weakness but as a strength that brings good things (Proverbs 22:4).
- our grandchildren resist seeking false greatness to fulfill their emotional needs (Philippians 2:3).
- our grandchildren see the greatness in serving (Matthew 20:28).

Heavenly Father, I confess that I have much to learn about meekness. Forgive my obsession with largeness. Teach me, Lord, to serve my family, friends, and neighbors with gentleness. Give me a heart to work behind the scenes and to celebrate the success of others. Help my grandchildren to take a stand against the cultural messages that invite them to seek greatness and power rather than service. May they find satisfaction in serving and in increasingly displaying the gentle and humble attitude of Jesus. Amen.

Think and Do

- Read Matthew 20:20–28. Where does this "obsession with largeness" reveal itself in our culture? Our homes? Our churches? What was Jesus' remedy for this problem?
- Richard Paul Evans' folktale *The Tower: A Story of Humility* illustrates for children the danger of thinking greatness comes from an exalted position.
- How can you be an example of meekness to your grandchildren? Is there anything you can change in your attitude, conversation, or actions that would demonstrate biblical meekness?

"Take my yoke upon you and learn from me, for I am gentle and humble in heart, and you will find rest for your souls" (Matthew 11:29).

"For by the grace given me I say to every one of you: Do not think of yourself more highly than you ought, but rather think of yourself with sober judgment, in accordance with the faith God has distributed to each of you" (Romans 12:3).

"How precious to me are your thoughts, God! How vast is the sum of them! Were I to count them, they would outnumber the grains of sand" (Psalm 139:17–18).

"Humility is the fear of the LORD; its wages are riches and honor and life" (Proverbs 22:4).

"Do nothing out of selfish ambition or vain conceit" (Philippians 2:3).

"Just as the Son of Man did not come to be served, but to serve, and to give his life as a ransom for many" (Matthew 20:28).

day twenty-three:
A WELL THAT NEVER RUNS DRY

Christ is not a reservoir but a spring.
A. B. Simpson

I thirst for you, my whole being longs for you, in a dry and parched land where there is no water.

Psalm 63:1

The well had been as dry as dust for more than thirty years. Decades before, it had been replaced by the miracles of city water and indoor plumbing. This reality did not keep my hopeful sister and me from relentlessly working the pump, longing to see just one drop of sparkling water. Hanging the aluminum can on the pump, we took turns jumping up and down, using our full weight, hoping to move the rusty handle.

Sometimes I sat on the cement slab at the base of the pump, eager to catch that one precious drop. If we had depended on this well to satisfy our physical thirst, we would have been in big trouble.

In my teen years we moved to a home in the country where there was no city water. Like many families, we did rely on a well. I cannot count the number of times the electric pump died. One summer the well ran dry without warning. We hired someone to dig a new one. But for days we were waterless! Imagine a home with three teenage girls and no water.

Water. We cannot live without it.

The Samaritan woman in John 4 understood this. So did Jesus. As He watched her lower her earthen jug into the ancient well, Jesus was aware of the even deeper spiritual thirst in her life—a hunger and thirst that only He could fill.

Like most of us, this woman had tried unsuccessfully to quench her own spiritual thirst. Unfortunately, all of her efforts were like trying to get water from a dry well. The harder she pumped, the thirstier she became.

Jesus offered to quench her scorching thirst forever.

Springs and streams wandering off the Ohio River fed the wells of my childhood. These wells required pumps.

Artesian wells are different. Water flows through layers of rock, becomes pressurized, and rises to the surface—it bubbles up. No pump needed.

Jesus said, "The water I give will be an artesian spring within, gushing fountains of endless life" (John 4:14 *The Message*).

Could it be that Jesus is our artesian well?

Of all that I pray about for my grandchildren, perhaps this is the most important: I pray that each of my grandchildren will accept the generous offer of Jesus to come to the Living Water. May His love bubble up and overflow into their lives and forever satisfy their thirsting souls.

Let Us Pray That . . .

- our grandchildren hear the story of the Living Water and understand the beautiful meaning of Jesus' words (John 4:10).

- our grandchildren hunger and thirst for righteousness (Psalm 143:6; Matthew 5:6).

- our grandchildren recognize the longings of their hearts as a longing for God and realize that only Jesus can fulfill those desires (John 4:26).

- our grandchildren understand that only Jesus can quench their thirst (John 4:13–14).

- our grandchildren will be satisfied in their relationship with God (Isaiah 58:11).

- our grandchildren remain in Christ and stay connected to the Living Water (John 15:4).

Living Water, it is true. Only you can quench our thirsting souls. Your water refreshes me, encourages me, and washes me clean. Thank you for the sacred water that you have promised will bubble up in anyone who comes to you. I pray that my grandchildren will come to you and never thirst again. May their search for satisfaction in life always lead them back to the Living Water. May they drink deeply and share the water with everyone who thirsts. Amen.

Think and Do

- John Piper has said, "God is most glorified in us when we are most satisfied in Him." If this is true, how do you exhibit your "satisfaction" with God? Are your grandchildren aware that you find your satisfaction in life through your relationship with Jesus?

- Much of the TV programming targeted toward children and adolescents sends the message that satisfaction comes from power, money, prestige, appearance, and physical attractiveness. They need our help and support to contend with the culture.

- Do you take the grandkids fishing? Sitting along a quiet stream provides a natural opportunity to initiate a gentle, spiritual conversation about Living Water with your grandchild.

"Jesus answered her, 'If you knew the gift of God and who it is that asks you for a drink, you would have asked him and he would have given you living water' " (John 4:10).

"I spread out my hands to you; I thirst for you like a parched land" (Psalm 143:6).

"Blessed are those who hunger and thirst for righteousness, for they will be filled" (Matthew 5:6).

"Everyone who drinks this water will be thirsty again, but whoever drinks the water I give them will never thirst. Indeed, the water I give them will become in them a spring of water welling up to eternal life" (John 4:13–14).

"The LORD will guide you always; he will satisfy your needs in a sun-scorched land and will strengthen your frame. You will be like a well-watered garden, like a spring whose waters never fail" (Isaiah 58:11).

"Remain in me, as I also remain in you" (John 15:4).

day twenty-four:
MERCY ME

What we are to others, God will be to us.
Charles Haddon Spurgeon

Blessed are the merciful, for they will be shown mercy.
Matthew 5:7

I would be lost without the mercy of God.

The Beatitudes are paradoxical. The poor in spirit become citizens of a heavenly kingdom. Mourners are comforted. The meek and humble inherit the earth. It is interesting that the promise to the merciful is slightly different. The merciful receive exactly what they have given—mercy.

Mercy receivers should be mercy givers. The reverse is true as well. Those who offer mercy with an open heart and open hand enjoy the limitless mercy of God.

I first became acquainted with Jean Valjean and *Les Misérables* while in language school outside of Paris. Victor Hugo's 1862 novel is a captivating story of pain, suffering, injustice, sacrifice, and mercy.

After Jean Valjean was arrested for stealing food, his heart was hardened and embittered by years of false imprisonment and harsh treatment. After Jean was paroled, desperate and filled with violent hatred, he made his way into a French village, where he faced rejection and insults as an ex-convict. Frightened and alone, he sought refuge in the home of a local clergyman, Bishop Myriel.

The bishop's household, noting Jean's harsh mannerisms and filthy, tattered clothing, viewed him with suspicion and fear. Ignoring an old women's warnings of impending danger, the bishop welcomed Jean into his home and shared the evening meal with him, using his finest silver to entertain the unlikely guest.

Before sunrise, the cynical and ungrateful Jean Valjean filled his sack with silver from the bishop's home. Fleeing through the countryside, the wretched man gave no thought to his crime. He thought only about making a new life for himself and enjoying the pleasures his stolen treasures would buy.

Back at the parsonage, the bishop's sister and their cook loudly lamented the loss of the silver and the old man's foolishness in trusting the criminal.

Within hours, the local gendarmes arrived at the bishop's door with the struggling Jean Valjean in tow. Showing the clergyman the silver in the sack, the officers accused Jean of thievery. Insisting that the man had not stolen the items, the bishop gave Jean his precious silver candlesticks as well. "These are a gift," he assured the officers and the astonished Jean Valjean.

The gentle bishop sent Jean on his way with kind words and a prayer that this gift of silver would enable him to live a different life, an honorable life.

The bishop's forgiveness expressed itself in an act of mercy.

It took many years, but the memory of this mercy slowly ate away at the bitterness in Jean's heart, freeing him to care for and love other people.

Mercy transformed the very soul of Jean Valjean.

I am a glad recipient of God's mercy. His tender mercy melts away the bitterness in my own stone-cold heart. I want to be changed into a generous, merciful, and forgiving person. I pray that my grandchildren will grow in their understanding of these qualities and will be mercy givers who take delight in the infinite mercy of God.

Let Us Pray That . . .

- we will be merciful in all our family interactions (Luke 6:36).

- our grandchildren understand their own need for mercy and God's willingness to give it (Luke 18:9–14).
- our grandchildren love mercy (Micah 6:8).
- our grandchildren will be grateful for the transforming power of God's rich mercy (Ephesians 2:4–5).
- our grandchildren show themselves merciful (Matthew 18:33).

Merciful Father, I thank you for the mercy you have showered upon our family. Help me to become a selfless mercy giver. Help my grandchildren on their own journey to experience your great mercy and love and to be transformed by your generosity. I ask that they would delight in your mercy. May they become known not only as objects of God's mercy but also as mercy givers. Help them to express your great mercy to those who do not know you. Amen.

Think and Do

- Do you recall a time when someone was merciful to you? What were the results of that expression of mercy in your life? How did being a mercy receiver help you become a better person? What were the effects on the mercy giver?
- It is often difficult to show mercy. Could it be because we have forgotten how much we need mercy ourselves? Read the parable in Matthew 18:21–35. What does this parable teach us?
- "Kyrie eleison" has been recited for centuries by faithful followers of Christ in the Greek Orthodox tradition. The phrase, which means, "Lord, have mercy" is both a request and an affirmation that God is merciful. How have you seen evidence of God's love and mercy toward you in the past week, month, or year? Who have you told about God's enduring mercy?
- Monica Kulling has written a children's adaptation of *Les Misérables*. Some children may find this book meaningful, and they may be inspired to become mercy givers.

109

"Be merciful, just as your Father is merciful" (Luke 6:36).

"God have mercy on me, a sinner" (Luke 18:13).

"He has shown you, O mortal, what is good. And what does the LORD require of you? To act justly and to love mercy and to walk humbly with your God" (Micah 6:8).

"But because of his great love for us, God, who is rich in mercy, made us alive with Christ even when we were dead in transgressions—it is by grace you have been saved" (Ephesians 2:4–5).

"Shouldn't you have had mercy on your fellow servant just as I had on you?" (Matthew 18:33).

day twenty-five:
HIDDEN SINS

He will easily be content and at peace, whose conscience is pure.

Thomas à Kempis

Who may ascend the mountain of the LORD?
Who may stand in his holy place?
The one who has clean hands and a pure heart.

Psalm 24:3–4

Doors of overhead compartments snapped closed. Passengers pushed, prodded, and squeezed bulky carry-ons under their seats. A disheveled young mother coaxed a reluctant toddler to take her seat. Flight attendants stocked their carts with honey-roasted peanuts and cold beverages. Tray tables and seats were locked in the upright position as required for takeoff.

Somewhat anxious, I placed a book on the empty blue-gray aisle seat beside me and craned to see over the seat in front of me, hoping to spot my husband before the "Fasten Seat Belt" sign was displayed. Passing through security had been uneventful for me but a hassle for him.

Although a frequent flyer, he had been pulled aside while I boarded the plane. Shoes off, standing in his socks with arms outstretched, my husband waited patiently as the Transportation Security Administration (TSA) agent waved his wand, searching for hidden weapons. Another screener rummaged through his briefcase and double-checked his boarding pass and ID.

Finally, airport security concluded that my husband posed no immediate threat to the plane or its passengers.

Airport searches are annoying but crucial to security. We have learned by tragic experience that hidden things can pose a horrific threat.

You and I can be professional "hiders." Dressing up in our Sunday best, we may carefully try to cover relational sins such as anger, hatred, pride, greed, self-centeredness, bitterness, jealousy, envy, lust, and distrust. Furthermore, we may resist searches that would expose these sins in us.

We may deny, rationalize, excuse, blame, and bury our wrongdoing. We may flee quietness where God can speak. We may tiptoe through Scripture to escape the pain of conviction. We carefully structure and dutifully go through our prayer list without pausing to listen. We select friends who will not challenge or expose us.

Some sins are hard to hide, however. Criminal behavior is difficult to conceal for long, and people generally condemn those sins. On the other hand, people tend to gloss over daily relational sins, such as impatience and resentment, as if they are as unimportant to God as they are to too many of us.

In Psalm 15 David asked the question, "LORD, who may dwell in your sacred tent? Who may live on your holy mountain?" And then came the answer: "The one whose walk is blameless, who does what is righteous" (v. 2).

David went on to provide a relational checklist for those who are blameless or pure in heart. The blameless person is someone who speaks with sincerity and honesty from the heart and does not indulge in slander and insults. He in no way harms his neighbors. He honors all God's people, keeps his word, and is generous in his dealings.

Too often, the opposite of these qualities—hurtful relational sins such as slander, insults, insincerity, dishonesty, breaking promises, and greed—are the exact sins we "hide." What we label as "little sins" can cause great harm to the people we love and can hinder our worship.

Facing our transgressions hurts! Confessing our sins is humbling and risky. It is so much easier to dress up, put on a little concealer and lipstick, and disregard our flaws.

David discovered the hard way that hiding his sins caused even greater pain than admitting them. "When I kept silent, my bones wasted away," he said (Psalm 32:3). David's hidden sins posed a horrific threat to his peace of mind, physical health, and relationship with God. Confession was his first step toward wholeness. It was the only step that could bring healing.

We need to examine our hearts for hidden sins and pray that our family members will welcome the "sin detector" of God's Word. "Blessed is the one whose transgressions are forgiven, whose sins are covered" (Psalm 32:1).

Let Us Pray That . . .

- our grandchildren willingly admit their sins and understand that when we confess our sins, God freely forgives (1 John 1:9).

- our grandchildren will be able to own their responsibility in conflict (Matthew 7:1–3; Romans 2:1).

- our grandchildren allow God to search their hearts (Psalm 139:23).

- our grandchildren will guard their hearts against sin (Proverbs 4:23).

- our grandchildren will hide God's Word in their hearts as a way of resisting sin (Psalm 119:11).

- our grandchildren will examine their hearts as part of their worship experience (1 Corinthians 11:28).

Heavenly Father, I am an expert at hiding my sins; I hide them even from myself. In your omniscience you are aware of all my sins and still love me. When I deny, rationalize, and excuse my sin, I only prolong my own suffering and create distance in our relationship. Humble me, Lord. I pray that my grandchildren will be honest about their sin. May they learn the benefits of examining and confessing their sins. Bring every sin into your light so they can find forgiveness and healing. May our family live with integrity and honesty and find the forgiveness we so desperately need. Amen.

Think and Do

- James 5:16 tells us to confess our sins to one another. Do you have a trusted friend in whom you can confide? Who is praying for your spiritual life? What role does confession play in your worship?
- We often gloss over relational sins. These sins hinder worship. Do you have relational sins you need to confess before Sunday?
- With the flavor of a folktale, *The Priest with Dirty Clothes* by R. C. Sproul teaches children about the total, complete, and indescribable forgiveness of Jesus Christ.

"If we confess our sins, he is faithful and just and will forgive us our sins and purify us from all unrighteousness" (1 John 1:9).

"You, therefore, have no excuse, you who pass judgment on someone else, for at whatever point you judge another, you are condemning yourself, because you who pass judgment do the same things" (Romans 2:1).

"Search me, God, and know my heart; test me and know my anxious thoughts. See if there is any offensive way in me, and lead me in the way everlasting" (Psalm 139:23–24).

"Above all else, guard your heart, for everything you do flows from it" (Proverbs 4:23).

"Everyone ought to examine themselves before they eat of the bread and drink from the cup" (1 Corinthians 11:28).

"I seek you with all of my heart; do not let me stray from your commands. I have hidden your word in my heart that I might not sin against you" (Psalm 119:10–11).

day twenty-six:
UNDIVIDED

When I have learnt to love God better than my earthly dearest,
I shall love my earthly dearest better than I do now.

C. S. Lewis

Give me an undivided heart, that I may fear your name.

Psalm 86:11

It started as most affairs do. A kind word here, a listening ear there—after all, they were just friends, nothing more than work colleagues. It was totally innocent. Eventually, casual lunches grew into intimate dinners where she poured out her anger at her husband, and he shared his disappointment with his wife. What began as sympathy and support soon developed into emotional attachment.

Evenings at their separate homes filled them both with anxiety. Distracted and dissatisfied, she went through the motions of preparing dinner and helping with homework. Constantly checking his phone for messages and impatient with the demands of family life, he made it apparent to his wife and kids that he longed to be somewhere else. Didn't he deserve a little happiness?

After hearts were broken, divorce papers were signed, custody was arranged, and lawyers were paid, they were left with little but regret and one nagging question: "How did this happen?"

The answer is simple.

They allowed their hearts to be divided.

She shared with someone else the affection that was rightly her husband's. He offered to a stranger the time, attention, and energy that belonged to his children and spouse.

Dividing our hearts never works.

Jesus tackled this issue with the Pharisees. "No one can serve two masters. Either you will hate the one and love the other, or you will be devoted to the one and despise the other" (Luke 16:13).

The pursuit of money quickly divides our hearts. The craving for status, power, possessions, comfort, or control distracts us and drains the life from our relationship with God. Seeking fulfillment and satisfaction in life while ignoring our relationship with God leaves us running in circles that go nowhere. Before long, our dysfunctional behavior inflicts pain everywhere we go.

One morning we wake up disconnected from God—empty and depressed. We are left with little but regret and nagging questions. "How could this have happened? How did I get here? God and I used to be so close." The answer is simple. We allowed our hearts to be divided. We shared with another the affection that is rightly God's. We gave to a stranger the time and energy that belongs to the Lord.

An undivided heart is an admirable goal for the remainder of our spiritual journey. An undivided heart is a precious prayer for our grandchildren's future walk with God. May they possess hearts fully fixed on Him.

Let Us Pray That . . .

- we search our own hearts and confess whatever threatens to divide them (Psalm 4:4).

- we recommit ourselves to Christ and are wholly devoted to Him (Matthew 16:24).

- our grandchildren will recognize whatever tempts them to wander from their commitment and divide their hearts (Mark 14:38).

- our grandchildren experience healthy relationships with role models who clearly have undivided hearts (Philippians 4:9).

- our grandchildren devote themselves to Jesus Christ throughout their lives (Psalm 27:4).

- our grandchildren turn to God's Word for guidance to nurture fully devoted hearts (2 Timothy 3:16).

- our grandchildren will guard against a divided heart in their own marriages (Genesis 2:24).

- our grandchildren experience the presence of God in their lives as they give their hearts completely to Him (Psalm 41:12).

- the world will be a better place because of our grandchildren's full devotion to Christ. "The world has yet to see what God can do with a man fully consecrated to him. By God's help, I am to be that man" (D. L. Moody).

Heavenly Father, it isn't that my heart is split in two; one part devoted to you and another part devoted to the world. The problem is that my heart is fractured, shattered into millions of pieces, each with a devotion to someone or something else. Forgive me for my broken and fickle heart, and help me put the pieces back together again. Give me an undivided heart. I pray, Lord, that my grandchildren will have the resolve to love you with all of their hearts and not to let anything subtract from their loyalty to you. May they be whole and holy people. May their devotion to you be unlike any the world has ever seen. Guard their hearts and keep them in the palm of your hand. I pray, Lord, that they may each be wholly devoted to you. Amen.

Think and Do

- "Life works when you recognize God has set His affections on us, and we set our affections on God" (Beth Moore). If this is true, how is life working for you today?

- The temptations that jeopardize our relationship with God can change with the ages and stages of life. What are your greatest obstacles to keeping an undivided heart in these middle and later years of life? How are you dealing with those challenges? In Daniel 1:8, Daniel had a plan for resisting the spiritual dangers of his culture. How can you connect Daniel's approach to your current situation?

- Luke 10:27 and Colossians 3:1–2 offer key insights into preserving our hearts. What safeguards will you put in place to keep your heart undivided?

"Tremble and do not sin; when you are on your beds, search your hearts and be silent" (Psalm 4:4).

"Jesus said to his disciples, "Whoever wants to be my disciple must deny themselves and take up their cross and follow me" (Matthew 16:24).

"Whatever you have learned or received or heard from me, or seen in me—put it into practice. And the God of peace will be with you" (Philippians 4:9).

"Watch and pray so that you will not fall into temptation. The spirit is willing, but the flesh is weak" (Mark 14:38).

"One thing I ask from the Lord, this only do I seek: that I may dwell in the house of the Lord all the days of my life, to gaze on the beauty of the Lord and to seek him in his temple" (Psalm 27:4).

"All Scripture is God-breathed and is useful for teaching, rebuking, correcting and training in righteousness" (2 Timothy 3:16).

"This is why a man leaves his father and mother and is united to his wife, and they become one flesh" (Genesis 2:24).

"Because of my integrity you uphold me and set me in your presence forever" (Psalm 41:12).

day twenty-seven:
QUIETNESS AND REST

Quietness allows room for God to speak or to be silent. Both are gifts.

Mark Buchanan

Then a great and powerful wind tore the mountains apart and shattered the rocks before the LORD, but the LORD was not in the wind. After the wind there was an earthquake, but the LORD was not in the earthquake. After the earthquake came a fire, but the LORD was not in the fire. And after the fire came a gentle whisper.

1 Kings 19:11–12

Quietness saturated Grandma's house. The tick of the kitchen clock, the hum of the ancient furnace, and the soft snoring of my grandmother at naptime were the only sounds I heard.

All was still.

The quietness carved out time to think, reflect, and pray. With time to enjoy solitude, I gazed out Grandma's parlor window and followed the ever-moving pattern created by sun filtering through the leaves of the red maple tree. Robins hopped through the long grass searching for worms.

Turning my attention inside, I noticed the sunlight streaming through the window, bringing new life to the faded, rose-patterned carpet. I took in each detail.

Evenings found my grandmother and me on the front porch for our nightly routine: watching the sun sink below the tree-lined hills. I'd stretch out on the porch swing with a glass of iced tea while Grandma occupied her usual spot in the green metal lawn chair. As night fell, the crickets tuned up for our entertainment. Conversation was not necessary.

My grandmother believed in God but rarely attended church. She did tell us the story of a summer at Hollow Rock Christian Campground and her memories of going forward at an altar call. A Bible and an *Upper Room* devotional booklet rested on the table next to her green recliner.

While my grandmother peacefully napped, I leafed through the worn black Bible and eagerly read the daily devotional. In the silence, God was tugging at my heart. Indeed, I had no one to talk to but God.

Now, I wonder, is quietness the absence of noise, or is it the gentle voice of God calling us to spend time with Him? Mark Buchanan, author of *The Rest of God*, believes there are "facets of God we discover only through stillness."

I have learned the pivotal lessons of life in quiet moments. It was in quietness that I received assurance of forgiveness. In quietness, I first came before God's throne. In quietness and reverence, I first worshiped Him. In quietness, I heard His call to serve.

Today, it is in quietness that I find peace when I am troubled. It is in quietness that I remember that God is sovereign. In quietness, I learn more of the mind of Christ. In quietness, repeatedly, I find healing for my soul.

When I am in trouble—emotionally, spiritually, or physically—I can often trace it to a lack of quietness and rest in my life. Quietness brings me strength. Rest bestows peace.

I am tired of the rush. I am tired of the noise. I am tired of the endless commotion and the unending demands heaped on us by affluence and technology.

It is time for some quiet, generous quiet, where we can experience God in ways that can only be appreciated in the stillness. I yearn to return to the silence of my grandmother's home, where all I heard was the soft tick of a clock and the gentle whispers of God.

Unfortunately, I cannot return to that quiet sanctuary. What I can do is create a tranquil sanctuary in my own home. I can encourage my grandchildren to take pleasure in Sabbath, to retreat from the hustle and bustle of life, and to simply be still.

Let Us Pray That . . .

- we learn the importance of periods of quietness and solitude (Isaiah 30:15).
- we learn to separate from the pervasive and widely accepted busyness of life to center on our relationship with God (Mark 6:31).
- our grandchildren begin to understand that rest can be found in God alone (Psalm 116:7).
- our grandchildren learn to embrace the spiritual disciplines of silence and solitude with Jesus as their example (Matthew 14:23; Mark 1:35).
- our grandchildren will allow themselves to cease from their work to acknowledge and worship God (Psalm 46:10).

Heavenly Father, I long to hear your still small voice. I need quietness. I need stillness. Save me from the rush, rush, rush of life. Help me to remove myself from the constant busyness that drowns out your voice. What I am doing as I dash from here to there is really not so important; listening to you is the priority of my life. Help my grandchildren to find those quiet moments when you will speak to them through your Word and through creation. May they make time alone with you their top priority. In those quiet moments, help them grasp the joy of your forgiveness. Reveal yourself to their hearts. May they find rest for their souls as they sit in your presence. Amen.

Think and Do

- We mistakenly believe that God speaks to us only through earth-shaking events. Read 1 Kings 19:11–13. When has God used a gentle whisper to comfort, instruct, or draw you closer?
- Do your grandchildren experience quiet moments in your home? Children often associate quietness with boredom. Teach them that quietness is alive with possibilities. Help them understand that quietness is not empty but can be

filled with creativity, daydreaming, planning, praying, worship, and appreciation for life.

- In Isaiah 30, God was speaking to His people, the Israelites, who were unwilling to listen to Him and were suffering the consequences. Isaiah 30:15 hinted at a remedy for the unique distress they were experiencing. Do you have distress in your life? Can you learn anything from God's exhortation to His people in this passage?

- *The Quiet Book* by Deborah Underwood uses endearing illustrations to help children understand the many different kinds of quiet they can enjoy each day.

"This is what the Sovereign LORD, the Holy One of Israel, says: 'In repentance and rest is your salvation, in quietness and trust is your strength' " (Isaiah 30:15).

"Then, because so many people were coming and going that they did not even have a chance to eat, he said to them, 'Come with me by yourselves to a quiet place and get some rest' " (Mark 6:31).

"Return to your rest, my soul, for the LORD has been good to you" (Psalm 116:7).

"Immediately Jesus made the disciples get into the boat and go on ahead of him to the other side, while he dismissed the crowd. After he had dismissed them, he went up on a mountainside by himself to pray" (Matthew 14:22–23).

"Very early in the morning, while it was still dark, Jesus got up, left the house and went off to a solitary place, where he prayed" (Mark 1:35).

"Be still and know that I am God; I will be exalted among the nations. I will be exalted in the earth" (Psalm 46:10).

day twenty-eight:
BEAUSOLEIL

Love precedes discipline.
John Owen

He cuts off every branch in me that bears no fruit, while every branch that does bear fruit he prunes so that it will be even more fruitful.

John 15:2

As we rounded the curve in the road, it was evident to our family that the residents had wisely chosen the name for this French village: Beausoleil, or "beautiful sun." The morning sun sparkled like diamonds on the blue-green surface of the Mediterranean, providing the villagers with a stunning view.

The thirty-kilometer drive from our home near Nice to the resort town of Menton ushered us along the French coast toward the Italian border. With the Maritime Alps on our left and with white sand and blue waters on our right, we were dazzled by both the natural beauty of the mountains and the charm of the white villas that peppered the hillside.

On our way to church we drove through four long, dark tunnels drilled through the mountains. As we came out of the blackness into the brilliant sunlight, we soaked up the beauty of hills drenched in gold. Vineyards were terraced into the rocky mountainside, creating a scene fit for the canvas of Monet or Cézanne.

Every Sunday we marked the progress of the vines. In the early spring, new branches wound around trellises. In the summer, the hills were decked out in vibrant green as the vines flourished. The fall brought a sight more spectacular than we could imagine as the purple grapes mixed with the yellow and red leaves. Our normally chatty family fell silent as we took in the beauty that epitomizes the South of France.

As we delighted in the incredible scenery and listened to worship music, we worshiped the Creator even before arriving at church.

The Mediterranean fall turned into gray winter. The once-lush vines began to fade and wither. One November morning, we were horrified to see dry sticks where our beloved vines had been. Where had they gone? Looking closer, we realized they had been pruned to stumps a mere two feet tall.

Hurrying into church, I tracked down Monsieur Bonicell, an older man who was always patient with my faltering French. "Monsieur," I pleaded, "what has happened to the grapevines? They are only stumps!"

My friend responded kindly, "*Vous ne comprenez pas, Madame.*" "You do not understand, Madame. The more severe the pruning, the greater the fruit."

Yes, I did understand. I should have remembered the John 15 teaching of Jesus about the Vine. "I am the true vine, and my Father is the gardener. He cuts off every branch in me that bears no fruit, while every branch that does bear fruit he prunes so that it will be even more fruitful" (vv. 1–2).

For days, I was deep in thought. I had experienced pruning before and knew there was surely more to come. Pruning is real and painful. As I considered what God had cut away in my life, I suddenly realized that what had been pruned away was not the complete story.

Whether the pruning happens to a person or to a grapevine, what is left is as important as what has been cut away.

With a mixture of joy and relief, I understood that all that was needed for the vines to climb the trellises of spring, to become the broad, green leaves of summer, to display the shocking yellow of the glorious fall, to be heavy with grapes, was still present.

In that stump of vine there was life.

Sometimes it seems that our lives have been chopped down to nothing. It is excruciating, messy, and never pretty. Yet, strangely, it is a good place to be.

When all is gone, the Vine remains. The Vine (Jesus) is our promise of spring, our promise of a vibrant and fruitful summer, the promise of a glorious fall and an abundant harvest.

When all is pruned away, it is all about who is left. And He is enough.

I do not relish future pruning. I am even less eager to watch my children or grandchildren go under the knife. However, protecting them or resisting their pruning is not a loving thing to do, for "the Lord disciplines the one he loves" (Hebrews 12:6). Pruning is always in our best interest and is the only way to be fruitful. "The more severe the pruning, the greater the fruit."

I need the divine Gardener's help to submit to discipline and resist the desire to intervene when those I love are being pruned and prepared for greater fruitfulness.

Lord, prune away!

Let Us Pray That . . .

- we willingly submit to the discipline of God (Hebrews 12:9).
- we see God's discipline in our lives and in the lives of our grandchildren as an indication of His love for us (Hebrews 12:6).
- God's discipline results in holiness in our lives and in the lives of our grandchildren (Hebrews 12:10).
- our grandchildren see God's discipline as a blessing in their lives (Psalm 94:12).
- our grandchildren will not despise the Lord's discipline (Proverbs 3:11).
- our grandchildren will not lose heart when they are pruned and disciplined (Hebrews 12:5).

- our grandchildren remain in the Vine and live fruitful lives because of the pruning they receive (John 15:2).
- our grandchildren understand they can do nothing apart from the Vine (John 15:5).

Divine Gardener, thank you for Jesus, the Vine. Thank you as well for the pruning you do to make the branches more fruitful. Lord, I pray that my grandchildren will be fruitful for your kingdom. I understand that a prayer for fruitfulness brings with it the certainty of painful pruning. May they submit to the work of your Holy Spirit. Clip away anything that is unhealthy or is a drain on their spiritual lives. Teach them the necessity of remaining in the Vine—the source of spiritual life and vitality. Amen.

Think and Do

- Even mature vines need to be pruned. When pruned properly, mature vines will produce a delicious and abundant harvest. Encourage your heart with the promise in Psalm 92:14 of a lifetime of fruitfulness.

- What is your attitude toward pruning? What do you need to abandon in your thinking to correctly view discipline as an indication of your Father's love? Do you fight pruning with complaints and anger? How can you realign your thinking so that pruning season prepares you for greater fruitfulness? Is there a gentle way to communicate this truth to your grandchildren?

- Nature is a wonderful teacher. Do you have rosebushes? Invite your grandchildren over on pruning day and teach them some horticultural (and spiritual) truths. Maybe a visit to a nearby botanic garden would provide opportunities for using God's creation to teach.

- Andrew Murray was a nineteenth-century South African pastor and a prolific writer. A devout Christian, he encouraged believers to remain in the vine, to abide in Christ, with these words: "All the vine possesses belongs to the branches." Rejoice in the life of Christ in you and consider ways you can be an example to your grandchildren of a believer who abides in Christ.

"Moreover, we have all had human fathers who disciplined us and we respected them for it. How much more should we submit to the Father of spirits and live! They disciplined us for a little while as they thought best; but God disciplines us for our good, in order that we may share in his holiness" (Hebrews 12:9–10).

"The Lord disciplines the one he loves, and he chastens everyone he accepts as his son" (Hebrews 12:6).

"Blessed is the one you discipline, Lord, the one you teach from your law" (Psalm 94:12).

"My son, do not despise the Lord's discipline, and do not resent his rebuke, because the Lord disciplines those he loves, as a father the son he delights in" (Proverbs 3:11–12).

"He cuts off every branch in me that bears no fruit, while every branch that does bear fruit he prunes so that it will be even more fruitful" (John 15:2).

"I am the vine; you are the branches. If you remain in me and I in you, you will bear much fruit; apart from me you can do nothing" (John 15:5).

day twenty-nine:
HEAVEN

Earth is receding; heaven is approaching. This is my crowning day!

D. L. Moody

My Father's house has many rooms; if that were not so, would I have told you that I am going there to prepare a place for you?

John 14:2

Our grandson Kevin has no memories of his father—our son-in-law Mike. Only eighteen months old at the time of his dad's accident, Kevin relies on pictures and the stories of family members to connect to his dad. When we laughingly tell him, "Kevin, that is something your dad would have done," he takes us at our word.

Nikki was four and a half when her daddy died—old enough to have memories of the early summer days just before his death. For a long time, she recalled a weekend trip she took with her mom, dad, and baby brother to the Wisconsin Dells.

When they returned, we quizzed our red-haired preschooler about her trip to the resort town. "What did you like best? Did you ride the 'ducks'? Did you like the shops? Did you bring us fudge?"

"Grandma, there was a swimming pool in the hotel. I went down the slide and Daddy caught me in his arms." At just the right moment, our daughter had snapped a picture of our son-in-law in the pool, at the bottom of the slide, with his arms outstretched ready to catch the squealing four-year-old.

We love that picture.

A trip to France was next on their summer agenda. An eight-hour flight with two little ones was exhausting. Undaunted, Jen and Mike were determined to enjoy every minute.

They visited the Eiffel Tower, wandered the streets of Paris, and ate *Petit Pain au Chocolat*. In the South of France, friends from our church embraced the young family and went out of their way to pamper "les enfants."

Our daughter was delighted to act as tour guide, leading her husband to her favorite restaurants to sample French cuisine. Even Nikki ate snails. They drove through the French countryside to explore a quaint village. It was the trip of a lifetime.

When we quizzed Nikki about France, her response was incredibly similar to the last time. "There was a swimming pool at the hotel, and Daddy caught me in his arms." So much for the Eiffel Tower.

In the weeks following Mike's death, our family, including Nikki, had countless conversations about heaven. One after-noon, after spending time at the pool, the little girl came to me with a question. "Grandma," she whispered, "are there swimming pools in heaven?"

I believe Nikki longed to jump into her daddy's arms again.

Over the years Nikki has developed an unshakable faith. She is convinced that God loves her and is preparing a place for her. For many years, when asked about her favorite Bible passage, without hesitation she would say it was John 14:2–3: "My Father's house has many rooms; if that were not so, would I have told you that I am going there to prepare a place for you? And if I go and prepare a place for you, I will come back and take you to be with me that you also may be where I am."

She believes that Jesus is even now preparing a place for her, and she has often wondered if He has invited her daddy to help with the construction.

We do not talk enough about heaven. It used to be true that Christians could be so "heavenly minded they were no earthly good." I could be mistaken, but I am wondering if the tables have turned. Are we so earthly minded that we have lost the joy and peace that come with the anticipation of our heavenly home?

I want my grandkids to have an understanding of the doctrine of heaven. I want them to know that the hope we have in Christ is real. I want them to know that they will be reunited with the people they love.

I want them to know that Jesus will be waiting for them with open arms.

Let Us Pray That . . .

- our grandchildren know that Jesus has promised us resurrection (John 11:25).
- our grandchildren understand that heaven is God's home and that someday He will make it our home as well (Revelation 21:3; 22:4–5).
- our grandchildren know they will someday be with Jesus in heaven (2 Corinthians 5:8).
- our grandchildren grasp the reality that there is no sorrow, pain, or death in heaven, and God shall wipe away all tears (Revelation 21:4).
- our grandchildren understand that heaven is a beautiful place prepared for those who love God (Revelation 21:11–27).

Father, heaven is your dwelling place. I cannot begin to imagine the beauty of your home. I also know that because of Jesus' death and resurrection, we will spend eternity with you where you are. I thank you for the joy and peace that fills my soul as I meditate on the reality of eternal life. Forgive me for speaking so little of the heavenly hope that we as Christians possess. I am thrilled that even if we are separated in this life, our family will be reunited in a land that needs no light, for you will be our Light. May my grandchildren's thoughts be filled with heaven. I ask that they would look forward in faith to all you are preparing for those who love you. May their hearts sing with the hope we have in Jesus Christ as they await their heavenly home. May biblical teaching on heaven be their comfort in times of sorrow. Amen.

Think and Do

- No more tears. No death. No pain or sorrow. Reunions with loved ones. Seeing God face to face. With all the treasures awaiting us, for what do you most long?

- As a child, what were your thoughts of heaven? Did you believe we would be floating on clouds or playing harps? What were your fears? How have you corrected your view of heaven?

- Study Revelation 21:11–27. What is your impression of these details?

- "Aim at heaven and you will get earth thrown in. Aim at earth and you get neither" (C. S. Lewis). How would changing your "aim" in life benefit you? Can you think of ways to focus more intentionally on eternity?

- Anne Graham Lotz's book for children *Heaven: God's Promise for Me* was written after the death of her mother, Ruth Graham Bell. Beautifully written and illustrated, this touching book provides answers and comfort to children who are wondering about heaven.

"Jesus said to her, 'I am the resurrection and the life. The one who believes in me will live, even though they die' " (John 11:25).

"And I heard a loud voice from the throne saying, 'Look! God's dwelling place is now among the people, and he will dwell with them. They will be his people, and God himself will be with them and be their God. "He will wipe every tear from their eyes. There will be no more death" or mourning or crying or pain, for the old order of things has passed away' " (Revelation 21:3–4).

"They will see his face, and his name will be on their foreheads. There will be no more night. They will not need the light of a lamp or the light of the sun, for the Lord God will give them light. And they will reign for ever and ever" (Revelation 22:4–5).

"We live by faith, not by sight. We are confident, I say, and would prefer to be away from the body and at home with the Lord" (2 Corinthians 5:7–8).

"I did not see a temple in the city, because the Lord God Almighty and the Lamb are its temple. The city does not need the sun or the moon to shine on it, for the glory of God gives it light, and the Lamb is its lamp. The nations will walk by its light, and the kings of the earth will bring their splendor into it" (Revelation 21:22–24).

day thirty:
THE SEA

Oh the deep, deep love of Jesus,
vast unmeasured boundless free!
Rolling as a mighty ocean in its fullness over me.
Underneath me, all around me, is the current of Thy love.
Leading onward, leading homeward
to Thy glorious rest above.

S. Trevor Francis

How wide and long and high and deep is the love of Christ.

Ephesians 3:18

We are drawn to the sea. It is wild, restless, and uncontrollable. We love its power, yet we fear it. Slathered with sunscreen, we recline on our beach blanket, enjoying our picnic lunch or building a sandcastle with our children, all the time keeping a safe distance from the thunderous beauty of the sea.

There are times when we cannot help ourselves. The call of the sea is strong, and we choose to venture closer. Rolling up our cuffs, we walk along the shore, admiring the beauty farther out but still only allowing the water to wash gently over our toes. The braver among us grab a raft and dash headlong into the sea. I watch with envy as the brave souls laugh with delight when a white-capped wave crashes against them and gently bobs them along. Some don scuba gear and examine the mysterious and beautiful world of the depths.

How I admire such bravery.

It might have been St. Augustine who first said, "God is a Sea." He is a Sea of limitless love and forgiveness. He is a Sea of acceptance and mercy. He is a Sea of strength and comfort. We love His power and we fear His power.

Strangely, I am tempted to keep a safe distance. I may roll up my cuffs and walk the shore of His love, but I avoid the depths. I am drawn to the Sea of God's love, but I am also tied to the shore by my own doubts, fears, anxiety, and misconceptions.

In *The Weight of Glory*, C. S. Lewis lamented his own struggle with the Sea. His picture of God as a Sea has challenged me. "This is my endlessly recurrent temptation: to go down to that Sea . . . and there neither dive nor swim nor float, but only dabble and splash, careful not to get out of my depth and holding on to the lifeline which connects me with my things temporal."[10]

So many of us, like Lewis, only dabble and splash. We do not know the delight that comes when we dive or swim or float in the Sea of God's love.

I am weary of my own fear, doubt, and caution. I am done with being tied to the shore where I build sandcastles that are so easily washed away.

I am so ready to dive in.

I am ready to plunge into the everlasting love of God. I am ready to swim, float, and dive if I need to.

I pray for the day when my grandchildren will set aside the building of sandcastles, leave their sunscreen at home, get off their beach blankets, and venture from the shore. I pray that they will dive into the Sea of God's love.

Let Us Pray That . . .

- we increasingly understand "how wide and long and high and deep is the love of Christ" and demonstrate that love to our grandchildren (Ephesians 3:18).

- we take the risk of believing in the infinite love of God (Psalm 103:11; 136:1).

- our grandchildren experience the everlasting love of God (Psalm 103:17).

- our grandchildren embrace the lavish love of God He offers to His children (1 John 3:1).

- our grandchildren understand that Jesus is the highest expression of God's love (John 3:16).

- our children will have the delight of leading their children to an understanding of the deep love of God and of becoming part of one endless line of faith until Christ returns (3 John 1:4).

Lord of Light and Love, my heart is drawn to your irresistible love and power, yet the unfathomable depth of this love frightens me. Forgive me for being so glued to my own comfort and fears that I resist diving in. Time and time again, I have missed the chance to delight in what it means to be loved by you. Lord, may my grandchildren be more adventuresome than I. I pray that they will risk leaving shore to explore the depths of your love. Help them set aside their own fears and love for this world so they can wade in without issues that weigh them down. As each year of their lives rushes by, may they grow more and more certain of your great love. May they be known as people who love and worship you. Amen.

Think and Do

- "God is love. He didn't need us. But He wanted us. And that is the most amazing thing" (Rick Warren). Meditate on the love of God as found in Scripture: Psalm 103:11; 103:17; 1 John 4:9–12; Romans 8:37–39; Deuteronomy 7:9. Which passage is most meaningful to you?

- In the classic *The Sacred Romance* by John Eldredge and Brent Curtis, we read that God not only saves us but He also woos us into a loving relationship. Think back on your life. Do you remember times when God was drawing you deeper into His love?

- *God Loves Me More Than That* by Dandi Daley Mackall enchants children with a description of the biggest, highest, and widest thing they can imagine—the love of God.

"And I pray that you, being rooted and established in love, may have power, together with all the Lord's holy people, to grasp how wide and long and high and deep is the love of Christ, and to know this love that surpasses knowledge—that you may be filled to the measure of all the fullness of God" (Ephesians 3:17–19).

"For as high as the heavens are above the earth, so great is his love for those who fear him" (Psalm 103:11).

"Give thanks to the LORD, for he is good. His love endures forever" (Psalm 136:1).

"But from everlasting to everlasting the LORD's love is with those who fear him, and his righteousness with their children's children—with those who keep his covenant and remember to obey his precepts" (Psalm 103:17–18).

"See what great love the Father has lavished on us, that we should be called the children of God! And that is what we are!" (1 John 3:1).

"For God so loved the world that he gave his one and only Son, that whoever believes in him shall not perish but have eternal life" (John 3:16).

"I have no greater joy than to hear that my children are walking in the truth" (3 John 1:4).

day thirty-one:
THE COURAGE OF LE CHAMBON

Courage is almost a contradiction in terms. It means a strong
desire to live taking the form of a readiness to die.

G. K. Chesterton

The LORD is my light and my salvation—whom shall I fear? The
LORD is the stronghold of my life—of whom shall I be afraid?

Psalm 27:1

During World War II, the mountain village of Le Chambon was
said to be the safest place in Europe for Jewish refugees. Driven
from their homes, stripped of belongings and livelihoods, ridi-
culed and trembling with fear, thousands of Jewish men, women,
and children sought shelter in the homes of the Chambonnais.

Convinced that life is sacred and resolved in their decision
to protect the Jewish people, the Huguenot Protestants of Le
Chambon-Sur-Lignon refused to submit to the cruelty and darkness surrounding them. Their defiance was demonstrated by
opening the entire town to the persecuted.

Every family in the village welcomed the displaced and terrified Jews. Schools were prepared to receive newcomers and
hide their identity. Farmers took on the arrivals as "workers."
Not one person was turned away.

When Nazi SS troops swarmed the town, the Jewish people
fled to hide in the countryside. When the empty Nazi trucks
rumbled out of town, residents of Le Chambon-Sur-Lignon
rushed to the countryside, using a song to signal to their Jewish
friends that they could safely return to the village.

The people of Le Chambon-Sur-Lignon made no attempt to conceal their sacred mission. Their resistance activities were well known by the German occupying forces and French collaborators. In a courageous and defiant letter, the leaders of Le Chambon explained their moral position to their adversaries. According to the author, Malcolm Gladwell, the essence of the bold letter to the Vichy government was, "We have Jews. You are not getting them."

The people of Le Chambon helped frightened refugees flee to Switzerland. Identity papers were created, names were changed, passports prepared, and plans made to escort those in the village's safekeeping through the hills to the border.

By the end of the war, this village of five thousand had saved the equivalent of its own population. Most of those who were saved were children. Not one person was lost.

Where did these farmers, shopkeepers, bakers, seamstresses, mothers, and fathers find the moral courage and grit to face down the Vichy government and defy the Nazi terrorists?

I wonder, if our family had been the village bakers in Le Chambon or farmers spending our days in the fields on the nearby hillsides, would we have welcomed a Jewish mother, father, or child into our home? How would we have responded to the opportunity to save an innocent person at the risk of our family safety?

Would compassion have overcome fear?

Would moral courage have given us the resolve to do what was right?

I want the moral courage and boldness of the citizens of Le Chambon-Sur-Lignon.

In 1990, Le Chambon was awarded the Righteous Among the Nations title by Israel. A small plaque honoring the village's humanitarian efforts in the face of danger was placed in the garden at the Holocaust Memorial in Israel.

Irish statesman Edmund Burke pronounced, "The only thing needed for evil to triumph is for good men to do nothing." It is unbearable to think that our lack of moral courage could permit evil to flourish or allow the innocent to suffer.

I want our family to have moral courage. I pray that every member of our family will find the strength to speak out against evil and to protect the innocent and persecuted—whatever the personal cost.

Let Us Pray That . . .

- our grandchildren will be quick to help the poor and rescue the oppressed (Psalm 82:4).
- our grandchildren will not harden their hearts to the needs of hurting and oppressed people (Deuteronomy 15:7).
- our grandchildren will not be afraid to take a stand against oppression and persecution (Jeremiah 22:3).
- our grandchildren understand the Christian responsibility to stand up for those being persecuted even to death (Proverbs 24:11).
- our grandchildren understand that God has placed them in the world for such a time as this (Esther 4:14).
- our grandchildren never show favoritism but see each person through the eyes of Christ (James 2:1).

Heavenly Father, I want to have the boldness of the citizens of Le Chambon. I ask that you would give to each member of our family true clarity in the issues of right and wrong. Please help my grandchildren to find the strength to do what is right even when difficult. May that strength come from knowing you are with them. When the opportunity arises, give them each the resolve of Daniel; the certainty of Shadrach, Meshach, and Abednego; the fearlessness of Esther; and the compassion of the French villagers of Le Chambon. May our family never stand by and watch evil flourish. Give us moral courage, we ask in the name of our Savior, who faced evil and won. Amen.

Think and Do

- When our oldest daughter, Jennifer, was very young, she loved the story of David and Goliath. She memorized a verse that was included in an audio dramatization for children, "Some trust in chariots and some in horses, but we trust in the name of the Lord our God" (Psalm 20:7). Read your grandchildren the stories of biblical heroes with moral courage: David, Joseph, Daniel, Esther, and others. Find corresponding Bible verses that reinforce the fact that moral courage is the result of trust.

- Read *Ruby Bridges Goes to School* with your grandchildren. Talk about the moral courage and faith of this little girl entering an all-white school.
- Did a grandparent or other family member fight in WWII? The Korean War? Vietnam? The Gulf War? Wars in Iraq or Afghanistan? Share pictures of this individual with your grandchildren and explain to them the moral courage it took for this person to do what was right to help protect innocent people.

"Rescue the weak and the needy; deliver them from the hand of the wicked" (Psalm 82:4).

"If anyone is poor among your fellow Israelites in any of the towns of the land the LORD your God is giving you, do not be hardhearted or tightfisted toward them" (Deuteronomy 15:7).

"This is what the LORD says: Do what is just and right. Rescue from the hand of the oppressor the one who has been robbed. Do no wrong or violence to the foreigner, the fatherless or the widow, and do not shed innocent blood in this place" (Jeremiah 22:3).

"Rescue those being led away to death; hold back those staggering toward slaughter. If you say, 'But we knew nothing about this,' does not he who weighs the heart perceive it? Does not he who guards your life know it? Will he not repay everyone according to what they have done?" (Proverbs 24:11–12).

"And who knows but that you have come to your royal position for such a time as this?" (Esther 4:14).

"My brothers and sisters, believers in our glorious Lord Jesus Christ must not show favoritism" (James 2:1).

day thirty-two:
IN GOD'S POCKET

When you cannot stand, He will bear you in His arms.
Frances de Sales

Cast all your anxiety on him because he cares for you.
1 Peter 5:7

Jesus was right. "Each day has enough trouble of its own" (Matthew 6:34). Even before we pry open our eyes, yawn ourselves awake, or rummage for comfy slippers, the day's troubles are whistling on our doorsteps.

Life has countless concerns: sick children, adolescents who struggle in school, job loss, broken appliances and broken relationships, financial agony, accidents and natural catastrophes, rejection, disillusionment, grim illness, misunderstandings, uncertainty about the future, loneliness, and grief.

Yes, "Each day has enough trouble of its own."

We met our Welsh friends Linda and Hedley Dent at Les Cedres, a French language school in a suburb of Paris. They had two young children, Fiona (4) and John Mark (2). Fiona and our daughter Joy were in the same kindergarten class at L'Ecole Maternelle.

At least once a week, the Dents would invite Joy for teatime. Linda and Hedley were playful and loving. One day, at tea, they served Joy snake's feet—radishes with butter. It took us a while to understand that they weren't really serving her snake.

The Dents worked in French churches for many years before returning to Wales. A rare liver disorder drained all strength from the tall, sandy-haired Hedley. Linda, a registered nurse, became his affectionate caregiver.

In June of 2009, Hedley went to heaven, leaving Linda, Fiona, and John Mark without the loving husband and father they cherished.

Hedley's death brought many challenges for Linda. Some days the ache was overpowering. Over time, she learned to honor and mourn the loss of Hedley while still enjoying the life she shares with her grown children.

She sings in a well-known Welsh choir. The group has recently released a CD of hymns. She works part-time in a Christian bookstore and in the summer often works as a volunteer at a Christian camp.

Together, Linda, Fiona, and John Mark weather the economic strains that so many in Wales are bearing. Through prayer, practical help, and laughter, they generously give one another love and support.

I recently asked Linda how she was doing. Hedley's birthday was soon approaching.

Without hesitation she replied, "I'm in God's pocket."

That is faith.

"Each day has enough trouble of its own." Linda's example has taught me that difficulties are not the only thing sitting on our doorstep.

Troubles may arrive early—but never too early for Jesus. He knows our needs. He knows our sorrows. He is there to comfort us. We are in His pocket.

My temptation as a mother and grandmother is to save my children from pain, sadness, sickness, struggle, and financial challenges.

In reality, I can't save them. Even if I could, it would be wrong for me to inject myself into their lives as their savior from all suffering.

The troubles of life can draw them close to God and strengthen their faith. May they never be cheated of the sweet experience of nestling in God's pocket.

Let Us Pray That . . .

- our grandchildren live strong and courageous because God is with them (Joshua 1:9).
- our grandchildren understand that God can use trials to increase their faith (James 1:2).
- our grandchildren believe that even the difficulties of life can work for their good (Romans 8:28).
- our grandchildren know that God cares for them and that they can cast all their worries at His feet (1 Peter 5:7).
- in the tragedies of life, our grandchildren will experience being carried close to the heart of God (Isaiah 40:11).

Dear Heavenly Father, thank you for going ahead of us and being completely aware of the troubles we face today as well as those we will be facing soon. When my grandchildren arrive at a day of trouble, may they also look for your presence. We know that you are already there and are not surprised by the struggles we face. Lord, I pray that as my children and grandchildren experience the countless difficulties of life, they will find their strength and comfort in you. May they make a conscious choice to stay close to you, to believe in you, and to rest in your pocket. Thank you, Lord, for my friend who has been a living example of trusting you in the midst of loss. Bless all those who, like her, are enduring pain and loneliness today. May you be their eternal comfort and great joy. I ask that you would be the comfort and joy of my children and grandchildren all the days of their lives. Amen.

Think and Do

- "You are my hiding place; you will protect me from trouble and surround me with songs of deliverance" (Psalm 32:7). In what life experiences did you know that God was hiding and protecting you? Can you write a short paragraph of that experience? Do your children and grandchildren know that piece of your story?

143

- Read one of the great picture books about pockets: *A Pocket for Corduroy, A Pocket Full of Kisses*, or *There's a Wocket in My Pocket*. Talk about things you can hide in a pocket. Then read Psalm 32:7 and tell the children that God can hide them and care for them.

- You may want to add two books about faith to your library. For younger children, you might enjoy reading *God Is with You: That Is All You Need* by Larry Libby. *Corrie Ten Boom: The Watchmaker's Daughter* by Jean Watson is appropriate for older children and can stimulate some important conversations about faith.

- Many adults struggle with their faith when they face difficulties. They wonder where God has gone. Help your grandchildren internalize the great theological truth that God is always with us, even in trouble. He never abandons His children to go through hard times without Him.

"Have I not commanded you? Be strong and courageous. Do not be afraid; do not be discouraged, for the LORD your God will be with you wherever you go" (Joshua 1:9).

"Consider it pure joy, my brothers and sisters, whenever you face trials of many kinds, because you know that the testing of your faith produces perseverance. Let perseverance finish its work so that you may be mature and complete, not lacking anything" (James 1:2–4).

"And we know that in all things God works for the good of those who love him, who have been called according to his purpose" (Romans 8:28).

"Cast all your anxiety on him because he cares for you" (1 Peter 5:7).

"He tends his flock like a shepherd: he gathers the lambs in his arms and carries them close to his heart; he gently leads those that have young" (Isaiah 40:11).

day thirty-three:
FULL-TIME LOYALTY

Jesus Christ is not valued at all until He is valued above all.

Augustine

I am the LORD your God, who brought you out of Egypt, out of the land of slavery. You shall have no other gods before me.

Exodus 20:2–3

Everyone holds allegiance to someone or something. It can take the form of patriotic feelings toward a nation or a commitment to a heartfelt cause. Most of us are loyal to our family, church, or workplace. Many swear an almost militant allegiance to a particular sports team. A few in our world are intensely loyal to their own self-interest and welfare, putting their personal wants and needs ahead of all others.

Loyalty is an amazing human strength. It calls up bravery, dedication, and focus in moments of peril. The most courageous acts in history have often been the result of the loyalty of a friend or the allegiance of a citizen. The world is a better place because of loyalty.

My grandparents were loyal people. My grandfather expressed family loyalty by providing necessities and using his carpentry skills in building and repairing homes belonging to family members. He ran a small business and had great loyalty to his employees and their welfare.

As a veteran of World War I, he demonstrated a great allegiance for his country. Near death with flu and pneumonia, he spent many weeks in the camp hospital. One night his lifeless body was placed on a front porch that served as a temporary morgue. Imagine the shock of the nurses when he called out to them the next morning. This soldier was very much alive.

My grandmother expressed her loyalty to my sisters and me as she shared her weekends with us, took us on a yearly shopping trip for school clothes, paid for dentist appointments, and played games. Without her help, I would not have been able to attend college. She passed away in 1979, but her quiet love and untiring support to her granddaughters is still remembered today.

In spite of the heartaches of the Great War and the struggles of the Great Depression, my grandparents were not bitter. Hardship seemed to increase their sense of loyalty. During World War II, both my grandfather and grandmother were involved in Civil Defense and were proud of their contribution. My grandmother's Civil Defense cap sits on a shelf in my bedroom.

Rezin and Rachel Morton were loyal and devoted citizens and loyal and devoted grandparents.

As heartwarming as loyalty to a country, a family, a cause, a job, or a friend can be, each person is called to a higher loyalty and a steadfast allegiance that is described in the first commandment: "I am the LORD your God, who brought you out of Egypt, out of the land of slavery. You shall have no other gods before me" (Exodus 20:2–3).

God begins the list of commandments by reminding His people of the unique relationship they shared. He was the One who brought them out of Egypt. He was the One who freed them from slavery. No false pagan god had cared for them. No man-made idol had set them free. God had shown His power and mercy on their behalf. There would be no excuse for turning to another worthless god.

Their love and devotion belonged only to Him.

The Israelites needed reminders of what God had done for them. Their allegiance and loyalty was to be based on their distinctive relationship with Almighty God.

We too need to remember who God is and all He has done for us, His people.

God is the One who created us and the vast universe.

God is the One who meets all of our needs.

God is the One who sent His Son to pay the penalty for our sins.

God is the One who sent His Spirit to dwell in us and guide us.

God is the One who hears and answers our heartfelt prayers.

God is the One who gives us true comfort in our loss.

God is the One who is preparing an eternal home for us.

God is the One who gives us His Word so we can know and love Him.

No one else, no country, no team, no friend, no job, no cause, and no relationship can ever do for us what God has done. Any attachment we turn to for comfort or in hopes of having our deepest needs met is a false god.

While many say they love God, their lives seem consumed with a loyalty to making money or pursuing happiness. Their loyalty is halfhearted. Their hearts are divided.

Almighty God has earned our complete allegiance and loyalty. In Vance Havner's words, "There is no such thing as part-time loyalty to Jesus."

My prayer is that my grandchildren will not only understand loyalty but will also have a full-time, unwavering loyalty to Jesus. May they always remember who God is and worship Him alone. May their allegiance be shown in worship, service, and obedience.

Let Us Pray That . . .

- each of our children and grandchildren will kneel at the name of Jesus Christ (Philippians 2:10).

- as parents and grandparents, we faithfully tell the next generation the praiseworthy deeds of the Lord so they too may know and worship Him (Psalm 78).

- our grandchildren understand that as followers of Christ they are to worship and serve Him only (Luke 4:8).
- our grandchildren will be God-pleasers (Galatians 1:10).
- our grandchildren follow Daniel's example and put their loyalty to God above all other loyalties (Daniel 6:10).
- praises to our God will be on our children's lips all day long (Psalm 35:28).

Heavenly Father, we owe you our allegiance and total loyalty simply because you are Almighty God. When we remember all you have done for us, our hearts are drawn to love you and serve you even more. We desire to have no other gods before you. We pledge our total allegiance to you. Cleanse our hearts of anything that would divide our loyalty between you and any other. We pray that our grandchildren will take to heart the first commandment and remember you as the God who saves them. May they never allow anything to hinder their full-time devotion to you. May their loyalty to you give rise to courage and determination to speak your Word. I ask that total allegiance to a loving God will permeate every area of their lives. Amen.

Think and Do

- Jim Elliot had a great allegiance to the Great Commission. He said, "He is no fool who gives what he cannot keep to gain that which he cannot lose." The story of Mr. Elliot's bravery, loyalty, and allegiance is one worth sharing with your grandchildren. You can read about it in Elisabeth Elliot's book *Through Gates of Splendor*.
- Do you have a copy of the Ten Commandments in your home? If you do, read them often with your grandchildren. Allow them to ask questions.
- Did you have a loyal friend in school? Can you share stories of loyalty from your own life? Take a few minutes to think of examples of loyalty and allegiance that you can share with your grandchildren at just the right moment.

"That at the name of Jesus every knee should bow, in heaven and on earth and under the earth, and every tongue acknowledge that Jesus Christ is Lord, to the glory of God the Father" (Philippians 2:10–11).

"I will utter hidden things, things from of old—things we have heard and known, things our ancestors have told us. We will not hide them from their descendants; we will tell the next generation the praiseworthy deeds of the LORD, his power, and the wonders he has done" (Psalm 78:2–4).

"Am I now trying to win the approval of human beings, or of God? Or am I trying to please people? If I were still trying to please people, I would not be a servant of Christ" (Galatians 1:10).

"Jesus answered, 'It is written: "Worship the Lord your God and serve him only" ' " (Luke 4:8).

"Now when Daniel learned that the decree had been published, he went home to his upstairs room where the windows opened toward Jerusalem. Three times a day he got down on his knees and prayed, giving thanks to his God, just as he had done before" (Daniel 6:10).

day thirty-four:
SAYING GRACE

Food cannot take care of spiritual, psychological and emotional problems, but the feeling of being loved and cared for, the actual comfort of the beauty and flavour of food, the increase of blood sugar and physical well-being, help one to go on during the next hours better equipped to meet the problems.

Edith Schaeffer, *What Is a Family?*

So whether you eat or drink or whatever you do, do it all for the glory of God.

1 Corinthians 10:31

Speaking at a meeting of the National Christian Counselors Association, the eating addictions counselor, Dr. Debra Giaramita, explained the emotional impact food had on her childhood.

As a member of an Italian family living in New York, she looked forward to weekends. Every Friday, she would join a horde of cousins who descended upon the love-filled home of their grandmother. As the grandchildren tumbled through the doorway, the aroma of onions, garlic, and bubbling tomato sauce greeted them. Grandmother, in her sauce-stained apron, instantly presented each child a giant meatball on a fork. The steaming mound of meat, spices, and marinara symbolized Grandma's love and kicked off two days of laughter and authentic Italian cooking.

Food is a gift. It is a gift from God that feeds more than our stomachs.

Food is an integral part of most celebrations. It was an essential part of the Old Testament festivals commanded by God. Turkeys, hams, cookies, and a variety of fun foods grace our holiday tables. We gather around the table not only to share the flavors, textures, and aromas but also to participate in community and feed our souls.

For many people, preparing new recipes and offering nourishing meals is a way of communicating love and care. Our heavenly Father first demonstrated this kind of love and care. He planted a garden for Adam and Eve. He provided them with every kind of tree—trees that were pleasing to the eye and were good for food. From the beginning, God designed food to bring nourishment and delight.

Sadly, many see food as a curse rather than a blessing. We eat too much. We eat the wrong things. We limit our diets to only what brings us pleasure, and we neglect key nutrients that God designed for our benefits.

Honestly, we all have overindulged to the point of discomfort and regret. Proverbs warns us, "If you find honey, eat just enough—too much of it, and you will vomit" (25:16). The possibility of eating to excess can be a source of temptation and distress.

Some people simply reject food. In pursuit of unrealistic thinness, hoping to cure the emptiness in their souls, thousands of young women reject food. Food, it seems, is the enemy.

For some, specific foods are the enemy. There is a growing tendency for people in search of health to be preoccupied with food by hyper-focusing on healthy choices. Certain foods are taboo. While their healthy choices are appropriate, their commitment to a definite diet can take on an almost religious fervor and consume every waking moment as they plan their next meal.

Whether it is overeating, using food to fill the holes in our hearts, mindlessly munching chips in front of the TV to counteract boredom, struggling with anorexia, or giving too much emotional energy to our food choices, the problem is the same.

We obsess over food. It consumes our thoughts.

There is a remedy for this sickness in our souls. It is gratitude.

In 1918, photographer Eric Enstrom of Bovey, Minnesota, met Charles Wilde. Captivated by the aging man's peaceful demeanor, Enstrom asked Mr. Wilde to pose for a photo. He agreed.

A bowl of gruel and a rustic loaf of bread sat on the table in front of the white-haired man. Mr. Wilde bowed his head and clasped his hands together in prayer. As he snapped the photo, Enstrom realized that this posture of gratitude was sincere and natural for Charles Wilde. Copies of the photo began to sell, and eventually Enstrom's daughter used the photo to create the painting we know today as *Grace*.

This painting, displayed in dining rooms across America as well as in other countries, captures an attitude of true thankfulness that warms our hearts.

There is freedom in acknowledging food as a gift. Receiving every forkful with gratitude and thanksgiving gives food its proper place.

God could have limited our options to mashed potatoes or steamed spinach.

Fortunately for us, He didn't. He provided us with an endless variety and enabled us to use our creativity to enjoy his gift in new ways.

First Timothy 4:4 tackles this issue: "For everything God created is good, and nothing is to be rejected if it is received with thanksgiving." Appreciation for God's gracious provisions isn't the total answer for food addictions, but it can be the first step on the road to a cure for our obsession with food.

My prayer is that my grandchildren's mealtime prayers will reflect a sincere appreciation for the good gifts God has given. I pray that whether they are savoring a meatball on a fork or dining on a simple meal of bread and soup, they will possess thankful and generous hearts that will worship the Giver and not the gift.

Let Us Pray That . . .

- our grandchildren see God as the provider of all of their daily needs (Psalm 104:14).

- our grandchildren spend themselves on behalf of the needy and hungry (Isaiah 58:10).
- our grandchildren know that God's love is sweeter and more satisfying than any food (Psalm 63:3–5).
- our grandchildren use self-control in this area of life (Galatians 5:22–23).
- our grandchildren receive God's gifts with gratitude (1 Timothy 4:4).

Dear Father, thank you for giving us our daily bread. We are truly thankful for the abundance with which you have blessed us. Thank you for not only giving us what we need but also for giving it to us in such enjoyable and beautiful ways. Forgive us for focusing on the gift rather than the giver. You are the source of all the blessings we receive, and we never want to forget that. Help our grandchildren to guard against obsession with food and to receive it with thanksgiving and responsibility. Teach our grandchildren that joy comes from sharing this gift with others who do not have enough. Move their hearts to care for the starving of the world and to make a significant difference. May our families be heard daily, giving thanks aloud for the gift of food that sustains and delights. May we never forget that Jesus is the Living Bread and only He can satisfy our souls. Amen.

Think and Do

- With younger children read *I Will Never Not Ever Eat a Tomato* by Lauren Child and talk about all the wonderful gifts of food.
- Read Genesis 1:29. How does this verse shape your attitude about food? Is there something you would like to change?
- Make a list of the foods for which you are grateful. Challenge your grandkids to do the same. Talk about our various preferences and celebrate the differences. Have a meal where a little of each person's favorite dish is served.

- Explore Christian websites that provide nutritional programs for children. Kids Against Hunger or Feed My Starving Children are two that can be very helpful. A trip to a packing station for one of these organizations can be life changing and may create a spirit of thankfulness in your grandchildren. Try supporting a child through a feeding program. Serve two or three times a year in a soup kitchen or food pantry. At Thanksgiving and Christmas, share canned goods and nonperishable items with your local pantry. Involve your grandkids in this project.
- Rethink your dinnertime prayer. How can it more fully express your gratitude for God's provision for your family? Write a family prayer of thanksgiving for God's gift of food.

"He makes grass grow for the cattle, and plants for people to cultivate—bringing forth food from the earth" (Psalm 104:14).

"And if you spend yourselves in behalf of the hungry and satisfy the needs of the oppressed, then your light will rise in the darkness, and your night will become like the noonday" (Isaiah 58:10).

"Because your love is better than life, my lips will glorify you. I will praise you as long as I live, and in your name I will lift up my hands. I will be fully satisfied as with the richest of foods; with singing lips my mouth will praise you" (Psalm 63:3–5).

"But the fruit of the Spirit is love, joy, peace, forbearance, kindness, goodness, faithfulness, gentleness and self-control. Against such things there is no law" (Galatians 5:22–23).

day thirty-five:
MI CASA ES SU CASA

Who covets more is evermore a slave.
Robert Herrick

Give me neither poverty nor riches, but give me only my daily bread.
Proverbs 30:8

Returning from a family funeral, the Springdale, Ohio, family received the surprise of a lifetime. Robert Carr had moved into their home and changed the locks.

Citing a "quiet title" and insisting the family had abandoned the home, Carr claimed the home as his own.

Long before Carr stepped foot in the rural Ohio home, he had already broken the tenth commandment. He desired something that belonged to another person and then acted to make it his own. This wasn't the first time the man had staked a claim on another family's residence. Authorities reveal he has filed "quiet title" paperwork on eleven other properties.[11]

This man may have a problem with coveting. He is not alone.

We have a covetous culture. We all want more of what we have. We want what we don't yet have. Some deeply desire the possessions of others.

Setting goals for a secure and healthy life is a positive thing. Dreaming of a comfortable home for our family seems appropriate. These desires can push a person to work toward a better

155

education, search for a new job, or to develop entrepreneurial skills.

This natural desire to care for our families crosses the line when we become obsessed with acquiring more and greater possessions through our own hard work or sometimes through the hard work of another person.

It is only fair to say that Robert Carr worked hard. It must have taken hours to file all the appropriate paperwork. Along with dozens of other people, he attended numerous seminars on how to pull off the scam. To the attendees of this bizarre seminar I would like to point out Exodus 20:17, "You shall not covet your neighbor's house."

Covetousness is an attitudinal sin. In no way does that mean it is hidden.

Covetousness can be seen in greed, selfishness, blame, envy, resentment, family breakups, jealousy, lack of empathy for the poor, thievery, stinginess, violence, trespassing, vandalism, and even in unrealistic demands for greater and greater benefits. We become slaves to the desire for more, and this desire robs us of the greater joys of life and our dearest relationships.

Covetousness is an ugly sin. It is an impoverishing sin. It is a form of idolatry.

Most concerning to me is that our society encourages covetousness. Anyone who has more than you have is your enemy. Anyone with a bigger house, nicer car, or better paying job is judged as greedy or selfish. Surely they didn't arrive at this place because of hard work.

It causes us to commit a mistake in our thinking known as "the fundamental attribution error." If others do well, it's because they were lucky. If I do well, it's because of hard work. If others fail, they must have been doing something wrong. They got what they deserved. If I fail, it's because life has not treated me fairly or I am under a spiritual attack.

We attribute good qualities to ourselves and bad motives to others. It is the antithesis of empathy, understanding, love, and grace; and it contributes to our covetous outlook.

The mindset of covetousness gives birth to a multitude of problems, demolishes relationships, tears down our own integrity, and threatens entire societies. But coveting also has a positive meaning we need to emphasize. Coveting can mean we have a deep desire for something good and noble.

I covet prayers for our grandchildren, that they would work hard, act responsibly, and learn to be content, generous, and grateful for what they have. May they never harbor resentment toward other people for their success or prosperity.

Let Us Pray That . . .

- our grandchildren rejoice with those who do well in life (Romans 12:15).
- our grandchildren understand the importance of hard work (Proverbs 12:11).
- our grandchildren live free of the love of money (1 Timothy 6:10).
- our grandchildren enjoy soul contentment whether they are rich or poor (Philippians 4:12).
- our grandchildren reap the rewards of godliness and contentment (1 Timothy 6:6).
- our grandchildren seek first the kingdom of God (Matthew 6:33).

Heavenly Father, I confess to you our own greed and preoccupation with material possessions. Forgive me, Lord, for times when I have looked on another's success or prosperity with envy or resentment. Teach me to rejoice with those who are doing well and to be generous with those who are struggling. Lord, I pray that you will put a "hedge" around the hearts of our grandchildren. Protect them, Lord, from this devastating and ugly sin of covetousness. Teach them contentment and generosity as well as the benefits of hard work. Guard their integrity as they deal with other people in the business of life. Lord, we know we have found our greatest riches in the person of Jesus Christ, and we thank you that it is well with our souls. Amen.

Think and Do

- One of the saddest stories of the Old Testament is found in 2 Samuel 11. David coveted Uriah's wife. The consequences were devastating. David's desire allowed him to justify behavior that was out of character for him. How does coveting cause us to act in ways that are out of the norm?

- Generosity is an antonym for covetousness. How can you encourage generosity in your grandchildren? How do you model generosity? *Those Shoes* by Maribeth Boelts can teach elementary-aged children the joy of generosity.

"Rejoice with those who rejoice; mourn with those who mourn" (Romans 12:15).

"Those who work their land will have abundant food, but those who chase fantasies have no sense" (Proverbs 12:11).

"For the love of money is a root of all kinds of evil. Some people, eager for money, have wandered from the faith and pierced themselves with many griefs" (1 Timothy 6:10).

"I know what it is to be in need, and I know what it is to have plenty. I have learned the secret of being content in any and every situation, whether well fed or hungry, whether living in plenty or in want. I can do all this through him who gives me strength" (Philippians 4:12–13).

"But godliness with contentment is great gain. For we brought nothing into the world, and we can take nothing out of it. But if we have food and clothing, we will be content with that" (1 Timothy 6:6–8).

"But seek first his kingdom and his righteousness, and all these things will be given to you as well" (Matthew 6:33).

day thirty-six:
LESSONS FROM THE FOG

I think that if God forgives us we must forgive ourselves. Otherwise, it is almost like setting up ourselves as a higher tribunal than Him.

C. S. Lewis

I have swept away your offenses like a cloud, your sins like the morning mist. Return to me, for I have redeemed you.

Isaiah 44:22

The dry remains of this year's corn crop poked through the black dirt. Dew covered the Wisconsin farmland on this harvest-time morning. A layer of fog floated over the empty fields like sheets on a clothesline.

As the October sun broke through the haze, the fog and mist dissolved before my eyes. It swirled and floated across the road in front of me, reminding me of smoke curling from a chimney.

Then it was gone.

Only the day before, I had meditated on Isaiah 44:22, "I have swept away your offenses like a cloud, your sins like the morning mist."

God does nothing halfway. His forgiveness is not available for just some of our sins or only for particular sins—but for all our sins. I am convinced that He does not cleanse us from all unrighteousness with the intention of allowing guilt to hang over us like a threatening cloud.

159

When we confess our trespasses, He sweeps them away like the morning fog. He puts them "behind His back," so to speak. He hurls them into the depths of the deepest sea.

Once we acknowledge our sins, it seems God is not interested in looking at them anymore.

However, we are. We ruminate on our sins. We examine and reexamine them. We cling to our shame as if suffering is the key to forgiveness. We allow our emotions to rewrite our theology, and our false beliefs loot our hearts of the freedom and joy that comes with God's tender mercy.

Who would we be as people of God if we took Him at His Word and believed that He has completely swept away our offenses? Would we have more power or a greater sense of mission if we believed that He has washed us white as snow?

I pray that my grandchildren will not travel through life with long faces and unresolved guilt, but with the freedom and beauty that absolute forgiveness brings.

Let Us Pray That . . .

- our grandchildren find freedom in Christ (Galatians 5:1).
- our grandchildren believe with all of their hearts that there is no condemnation for the followers of Jesus Christ (Romans 8:1).
- our grandchildren believe that God chooses to remember their sins no more (Isaiah 38:17).
- our grandchildren believe that their sins are gone, gone, gone (Psalm 103:12).
- our grandchildren will not live with shame and guilt but look to Christ for forgiveness (Psalm 34:5).

Heavenly Father, I thank you for the countless ways you speak to us in your creation. I praise you for the lesson of the morning mist. No words can express my gratitude for the perfection of your forgiveness. Thank you, Lord, for the complete forgiveness that is offered in Jesus Christ. May my grandchildren not fall victim to unnecessary guilt or doubt about your ability to forgive. May they rejoice in the power of the blood of Jesus Christ to wipe the slate clean! Lord, may this next generation be a generation of forgiven ones, living in complete freedom and experiencing the joy of their salvation. May they carry to the ends of the earth the good news of our God, who completely forgives our sins! Amen.

Think and Do

- Do you live by the ocean? Or one of the Great Lakes? If you do, next time the grandkids visit and fog is in the forecast, wrap up in your windbreakers and sit along the shore. Your grandkids will be fascinated as the mist rolls in. If the sun breaks through and the fog begins to melt away, share Isaiah 44:22 with them. Low-lying areas in other parts of the country can have pockets of fog that are great illustrations of this verse. Be on the lookout for the opportunity to use God's creation and God's Word together.

- For middle schoolers, a science experiment with fog is a great way to open this discussion. Fog experiments generally involve boiling water, so grandparent supervision is required.

- *Hide and Seek Fog* by Alvin Tresslet and Roger Duvoisin will help children who have little experience with fog. Fog settles on a seaside village for days. When the sun finally melts the mist away, villagers can continue life as usual.

- When your grandchild disobeys, consider it an opportunity to open God's Word for them. Be ready with some of the beautiful illustrations of forgiveness we find in Scripture. Ask them for their thoughts on terms such as "swept away," "blotted out," "cast into the depths," "trampled upon," and "remembered no more." Allow them to illustrate their favorite word picture for forgiveness.

- Is there some sin in your past that you fear is too dreadful to be forgiven? Allow God to sweep it away like the morning mist.

"It is for freedom that Christ has set us free. Stand firm, then, and do not let yourselves be burdened again by a yoke of slavery" (Galatians 5:1).

"Therefore, there is now no condemnation for those who are in Christ Jesus, because through Christ Jesus the law of the Spirit who gives life has set you free from the law of sin and death" (Romans 8:1–2).

"You have put all my sins behind your back" (Isaiah 38:17).

"Those who look to him are radiant; their faces are never covered with shame" (Psalm 34:5).

"As far as the east is from the west, so far has he removed our transgressions from us" (Psalm 103:12).

day thirty-seven:
BARISTAS AND THE GOLDEN RULE

We have committed the Golden Rule to memory; let us now commit it to life.

Edwin Markham

So in everything, *do to others* what you would have them *do to you*, for this sums up the Law and the Prophets.

Matthew 7:12

Twenty-year-old Colton Ryan Gleason, who was in his third year at Minnesota State University, worked in the family business. On September 20, 2012, he was walking through an alleyway with a group of friends when a mid-sized car pulled up next to him. A young man jumped from the car and without warning punched Colton in the head. Colton died at 9:15 p.m. His assailant was only seventeen years old.[12]

The "knockout game" is not isolated to Minnesota. In New Jersey, a man was struck so hard that his neck was broken. A Pittsburgh teacher was knocked out as he walked home from school. In St. Louis, a seventy-two-year-old Vietnamese immigrant, Hoang Nguyen, died after stepping in front of a group of teens to protect his wife.

The players of this game often share videos of the event and are seen laughing and celebrating that they are the "knockout kings."

This so-called game is not the only problem. Bullying has exploded in schools and the work place. Anti-bullying programs, initiated with the best of intentions, have made little difference. The aggression, violence, and spiritual poverty of our culture have damaged the souls of our children. Nothing will change until we heal these wounds.

Growing up in the 1950s and 1960s, I was aware there were bullies at school. Generally, discipline was swift and effective. Neighbors kept a close eye on all the children, and when a bully would emerge the tormentor was promptly sent home. Teachers escorted bullies from classrooms until such a time as they could correct their behavior. Bus drivers reported intimidators to the school office and defended smaller victims. Embarrassed parents lectured and restricted the offenders. Classmates frequently isolated the bully, not wanting to be associated with his deeds.

It certainly wasn't a trouble-free time, but there existed an understanding in the culture that taught even the youngest child this truth: It is wrong to physically harm other people. Cruelty will not be tolerated.

Everyone knew the Golden Rule.

In our home, squabbling with my sisters was common. Whose turn was it to do the dishes? Take out the dog? Fold the laundry? Wear a special outfit? We were normal kids.

Every time we argued, the Golden Rule came to mind. I may not have acted upon it, but I found this positive teaching from Scripture inescapable.

Everywhere, we heard the words of Jesus that we have come to know as the Golden Rule. We heard it from our parents. We picked it up from our grandparents, great-aunts, and uncles. It was repeated at school, in the neighborhood, and at church. "Do unto others as you would have them do unto you."

There are no simple answers to the ills of our society, but the Golden Rule provides the basics we can teach even the youngest child. If they want kindness, they should treat others with kindness. If they yearn to be understood, they should learn to be understanding. If they desire respect, they should first give respect to family and friends. If they want forgiveness, they must learn to forgive.

Homes, neighborhoods, schools, churches, and workplaces would be revolutionized if we were to treat everyone with the kindness and respect we want for ourselves. Transformation always occurs when the words of Jesus are taken to heart.

We seldom hear people teaching the principles of the Golden Rule, the Sermon on the Mount, or the Beatitudes anymore. Our world has largely abandoned these guardrails that kept us from running off the road and into dangerous territory.

It isn't hopeless.

I enjoy our local coffee shops that are staffed by college-aged baristas. They greet me each time I enter the store. The young ladies ask me about my day. One young man even remembers that I babysit my grandkids. They seem to look past my graying hair and frequent confusion over what to order. While they may not be using the Golden Rule as their guide, their corporate offices have created a culture of kindness and respect among their employees, and it works. I keep going back.

I appreciate the kindness and respect of these young people. It is a good trend, and it gives me hope. Someday the kindness of these young people will outweigh the violence that has erupted in our culture.

In the meantime, we can begin a revival of Jesus' teaching: "Do to others what you would have them do to you" (Matthew 7:12). We can create a culture of respect by treating every generation with the dignity and kindness we crave for ourselves.

I pray that my grandchildren will take to heart the teachings of Jesus. May they remember to treat family members, friends, teachers, colleagues, and employers with the same kindness and respect they would like to receive.

Let Us Pray That . . .

- our grandchildren are kind and tenderhearted (Ephesians 4:32).

- our grandchildren show respect for older people (Leviticus 19:32).

- our grandchildren reject violence (Proverbs 3:31).

- our grandchildren reject favoritism and treat each person with dignity (Romans 2:11).
- our grandchildren understand that every person is made in the image of God (Genesis 5:1–2).
- our grandchildren will be familiar with and obey the "one another" commands of the New Testament.

Heavenly Father, my heart aches when I see the brokenness of many young people in our country. It is obvious that many of them lack respect for others because they have not received it themselves. Father, heal their wounds. Draw them to yourself for the healing that only your love can bring. Satisfy their souls with the adventure of loving you. Teach us how to deal with our own children and grandchildren in a respectful way and to hold them accountable for being respectful in return. May your words, "Do to others as you would have them to do to you" find a resting place in their hearts and lead to kind and caring behavior. May they embrace the concept of individual dignity and make a difference not only with their loved ones but also with whomever they meet. I ask that this next generation would be rich in acts of kindness that reflect your great love for the world. Amen.

Think and Do

- *Have You Filled a Bucket Today?* by Carol McCloud effectively teaches children that their words and actions can help other people feel better. Challenge your grandchildren to find ways to fill some buckets today. Be certain to remind them that the kind words and actions of other people can make them feel loved, but only Jesus can completely fill them up.
- Visit a nursing home with your grandchildren. Allow them to take small gifts to the residents and to interact. Teach them that showing respect for the elderly is taught in the Bible.
- Is your grandchild being bullied? What can you do to fill his or her bucket so that the cruel words and actions are

less painful? Pray for your grandchild and pray that Mom and Dad will have wisdom in dealing with the situation.

"Be kind and compassionate to one another, forgiving each other, just as in Christ God forgave you" (Ephesians 4:32).

"Stand up in the presence of the aged, show respect for the elderly and revere your God. I am the LORD" (Leviticus 19:32).

"Do not envy the violent or choose any of their ways" (Proverbs 3:31).

"For God does not show favoritism" (Romans 2:11).

"When God created mankind, he made them in the likeness of God. He created them male and female and blessed them" (Genesis 5:1–2).

"Accept one another, then, just as Christ accepted you, in order to bring praise to God" (Romans 15:7).

"Be devoted to one another in love. Honor one another above yourselves" (Romans 12:10).

"Finally, all of you, be like-minded, be sympathetic, love one another, be compassionate and humble" (1 Peter 3:8).

day thirty-eight:
ROUNDABOUTS

The way he makes for us is his way, not ours.
Henry Cloud

I will instruct you and teach you in the way you should go;
I will counsel you with my loving eye on you.
Psalm 32:8

A dozen Parisian streets converge at Place Charles de Gaulle. Vehicles from boutique-lined avenues zip into the ten unmarked lanes of traffic that circle the Arc de Triomphe. This is the champion of all roundabouts.

Linger on the observation deck of the nearby Eiffel Tower, and you will make out the starlike pattern formed by the meeting of these chic streets. At night, the combination of city lights and car lights illuminate the intersection known to Parisian residents as L'Etoile—The Star.

At street level, photographers use time-lapse photography to capture streaks of light from speeding cars. Undoubtedly, their framed photography decorates the walls of posh apartments in this fashionable section of the City of Lights.

Driving in Paris is a challenge. L'Etoile is one of the most dangerous intersections in the world. Tire-squealing mini-coupes, brave bicyclists, puttering mopeds, daredevil motorcyclists, and the ever-present tourist buses dart in and out as they struggle to reach their destination. It is hair-raising and disorienting.

Some years, the Tour de France has ended with the riders taking a lap around this famous circle.

For our thirteen-year-old son, a lap around L'Etoile was as thrilling as a roller coaster ride. As my husband did his best to preserve our lives, I dug my nails into the armrest of our gray Peugeot, and the three girls squealed in the back. When traffic was especially heavy, it might take more than one trip around L'Etoile to get to our desired street. Our son did not mind. "One more time, Dad!" he would shout. "One more time."

Roundabouts can be fun. They can also keep us from reaching our destination.

All of us have taken a few extra laps around an unhealthy relationship or dead-end job. Sometimes we twirl and dance around the same old grievances or hurts. We refuse to exit to a healthier avenue of thinking.

Young people can get caught in the revolving door of regret or a dizzying orbit of fear of the future. When they gyrate around the false belief that they have no choices in life, they come dangerously close to adopting a victim mentality.

Exiting a difficult relationship, a meaningless job, or a negative way of thinking and relating is very difficult, but necessary.

It is inevitable that our grandchildren will sometimes be caught up in the speed and excitement of life and find they are going in a direction that is keeping them from their desired destination. My prayer is that they will have the courage to put on the brakes, take the best exit, and find a direction that will lead them closer to God.

Let Us Pray That . . .

- our grandchildren sincerely believe that God has plans for their future (Jeremiah 29:11).

- our grandchildren follow as God guides them in paths of righteousness (Psalm 23:3).

- our grandchildren call out to God for help when they lack wisdom (James 1:5).

- our grandchildren seek out wise counselors (Proverbs 11:14).

- our grandchildren trust that God can and will direct their steps (Psalm 37:23).

- our grandchildren understand the personal nature of God's guidance (Psalm 32:8).

Heavenly Father, sometimes we all allow life to carry us along. Before we know it, we are far from where you want us to be. Lord, help my grandchildren to live thoughtfully and intentionally. May they catch a glimpse of the destination you have planned for them—a destination with healthy relationships, meaningful and responsible work, and the ability to make a contribution to your kingdom. When they don't know how to get back on the right path, would you show them how to self-correct and make the changes that are necessary to live an abundant life? May your Word be their constant guide and companion. Amen.

Think and Do

- Read Psalm 25. Note how many times the psalmist asks God to teach him to walk in His path. Can you use any of the verses to write a prayer requesting God's guidance for your grandchildren?

- Geocaching is a great family activity. Geocaching allows you to get your kids outdoors and requires them to follow the directions of the specially designed GPS as you enjoy this unique scavenger hunt. There are geocaching sites online that can help you choose kid- and grandma-friendly searches close to home. Always carry insect repellant and a fully charged phone. Go with another family. Do some research. It is a wonderful opportunity to draw a comparison between finding the right path for your hunt and finding God's path for their lives.

- Jeremiah 29:11 is a verse we often use at high school graduations. This promise was given by God to His people in exile to reassure them that He still had a plan for them. While it was written directly to the Israelites, it gives a glimpse into the nature of God. What can you learn from this verse that is an encouragement and comfort?

" 'For I know the plans I have for you,' declares the LORD, 'plans to prosper you and not to harm you, plans to give you hope and a future' " (Jeremiah 29:11).

"The LORD is my shepherd, I lack nothing. He makes me lie down in green pastures, he leads me beside quiet waters, he refreshes my soul. He guides me along the right paths for his name's sake" (Psalm 23:1–3).

"If any of you lacks wisdom, you should ask God, who gives generously to all without finding fault, and it will be given to you" (James 1:5).

"The LORD makes firm the steps of the one who delights in him; though he may stumble, he will not fall, for the LORD upholds him with his hand" (Psalm 37:23-24).

"I will instruct you and teach you in the way you should go; I will counsel you with my loving eye on you" (Psalm 32:8).

day thirty-nine:
"ATHEISTS DON'T HAVE NO SONGS"

In almost everything that touches our everyday life on earth, God is pleased when we are pleased. He wills that we be as free as birds to soar and sing our maker's praise without anxiety.

A. W. Tozer

I will sing to the LORD all my life; I will sing praise to my God as long as I live.

Psalm 104:33

Whitening. Tartar control. Breath-freshening. Anti-gingivitis. So many choices. I wondered if life wouldn't be simpler and less confusing without all of these options. Frozen in front of the toothpaste display, I was suddenly distracted by a thin, female voice singing a scratchy rendition of a Frank Sinatra tune.

Pushing my cart around the end of the aisle, I spotted an elderly, white-haired woman swaying back and forth on a bench near the prescription pick-up window. Disheveled and with eyes closed, she looked like someone who had been deposited on the bench while her caregivers tried on shoes or checked out the Blue Light Special.

Then her eyes fluttered open, and for just a moment our gaze met. I was chilled by the pain and loneliness I saw. Seemingly unmoved by the human connection, she closed her eyes once again and retreated into her own world, perhaps to dream of

172

dancing and swaying in the arms of an old love as they listened to Sinatra.

Her song was the song of lost love, loneliness, and regret.

As quickly as possible, I turned my cart down the next aisle, hoping to remove myself from the heartbreaking and embarrassing scene. My purchases that day—ultra hydrating lotion, Tylenol for my backache during the day, Tylenol PM to sleep at night, assorted brands of antacids—reminded me that my turn to be deposited on a bench could be here sooner than I would like.

I remember another woman.

I was only sixteen or seventeen. I lingered in the hallway of St. John's Hospital, waiting for my candy striper sister to be done with her work for the day. The hall was glowing with light and warmth as the afternoon sun reflected off the freshly cleaned and polished floors. Fingering a magazine on a nearby cart, I was in a hurry to leave and hoped my sister would soon appear.

My impatient thoughts were interrupted by the sound of a weak female voice singing a scratchy rendition of a song our choir was rehearsing for our upcoming high school concert.

Where was that melody coming from? Turning, I noticed that the door to the room behind me was slightly ajar. As I peeked into the room, I saw a tiny, frail, white-haired woman under a white sheet. Unaware that she was being watched, she continued her song: "Bless thou the LORD, O my soul. And all that is within me bless His holy name. He is full of compassion and mercy. Longsuffering and great in goodness . . . Bless thou the LORD, O my soul."

I backed away from the door. I was eavesdropping on a holy and important conversation.

This elderly woman's song was a song of love, gratitude, and comfort because she knew she was not alone. Even after fifty years, I still can recall the peace and faith she expressed while singing from a hospital bed.

Two women. Two songs. For years, each had engaged in daily rehearsals. One score was written with the ink of despair and disappointment. The other was written with strokes of gratitude and hope.

As I left the store, it occurred to me that I too am engaging in daily rehearsals. I choose each day whether to sing a song of faith or a song of despair. My reactions to life's disappointments and my ability to cope with the physical and emotional changes that will inevitably come my way contribute to the beauty or the melancholy-filled tone of the composition.

Today and tomorrow and all the days yet to come, I have the opportunity to rehearse the song I will be crooning as I sit on a bench by the prescription window or lie in a hospital bed.

I choose to sing a song of faith.

Comedian and banjo player Steve Martin has written a song entitled "Atheists Don't Have No Songs." Martin introduces the song by reminding his audience of the wealth of beautiful music written and enjoyed by people of faith. Holding up a single sheet of paper, he announces, "This is the atheist hymnal." He then proceeds to sing the first verse, which mentions that Christians, Jews, and Baptists have various kinds of songs. Then he concludes that stanza by saying that all the atheists have to sing are the blues.

Our hearts are saddened when we realize that so many people in the world have no song to sing except the blues. My prayer is that I will sing a song of faith all the days of my life. I ask the Lord to make me an example of grace and gratitude as I age. I pray that God will fill my grandchildren's hearts until they burst with songs of joy and peace.

Let Us Pray That . . .

- God puts a new song in our hearts (Psalm 40:3).
- we sing to the LORD for as long as we live and leave our grandchildren an example (Psalm 104:33).
- our grandchildren's hearts will sing, and they will not be silent (Psalm 30:12).
- our grandchildren sing for joy (Psalm 95:1).
- our grandchildren use music to encourage others (Ephesians 5:19).
- our grandchildren are present when the great multitude from all tribes and nations cry out, "Salvation belongs to our God, who sits on the throne, and to the Lamb" (Revelation 7:10).

Giver of Music, thank you for the songs of the birds that announce the coming of spring. Thank you for the melody of a gentle brook and the pleasing laughter of children. Your word tells me that even the stars sing to you. All creation sings your praise. Father, I ask that you would soften my heart until there is a song of peace and joy on my lips. I choose to spend each day rehearsing the song of my life—a song of love to you. Forgive me for the countless days when I lose focus, forget the joyful tune, and sing a dirge instead. I pray that my grandchildren will choose a song of faith, gratitude, hope, and peace as they walk through life. Help them to understand that it is never too early to practice singing your praise. Amen.

Think and Do

- Two women. Two songs. One song was filled with joy and hope. The other song was filled with sadness and loneliness. Which song best describes the song you are singing today? Is there a hymn or worship song you could choose that would exemplify the song you would like to sing?

- When our granddaughter Nicole was very young, her paternal grandfather taught her a song. It was one that her daddy loved when he was a little boy. Do you know this children's song? Do you have a sweet song to teach your grandchildren?

> The birdies in the treetops
> sing their song;
> The angels chant their chorus
> all day long;
> The flowers in the garden
> blend their hue,
> So why shouldn't I,
> Why shouldn't you,
> Praise Him too?

- In the fall of 2001, after the horrible events of 9/11 and a tragedy in the life of one of our children, I found getting up in the morning to be nearly impossible. It was hard to face the day when I considered all the pain that was being experienced by so many others. A friend suggested I memorize Psalm 103. I began to memorize the wonderful words that begin, "Praise the LORD, my soul." That psalm, mingled with the memory of the song I heard so long ago in a hospital corridor, became my morning routine. Before long, hope returned. Can you find a similar psalm to be your morning song of faith?

"He put a new song in my mouth, a hymn of praise to our God. Many will see and fear the LORD and put their trust in him" (Psalm 40:3).

"I will sing to the LORD all my life; I will sing praise to my God as long as I live" (Psalm 104:33).

"You turned my wailing into dancing; you removed my sackcloth and clothed me with joy, that my heart may sing your praises and not be silent. LORD my God, I will praise you forever" (Psalm 30:11–12).

"[Speak] to one another with psalms, hymns, and songs from the Spirit. Sing and make music from your heart to the Lord, always giving thanks to God the Father for everything, in the name of our Lord Jesus Christ" (Ephesians 5:19–20).

"After this I looked, and there before me was a great multitude that no one could count, from every nation, tribe, people and language, standing before the throne and before the Lamb. They were wearing white robes and were holding palm branches in their hands. And they cried out in a loud voice: 'Salvation belongs to our God, who sits on the throne, and to the Lamb' " (Revelation 7:9–10).

day forty:
THE RIGHT PERSON

Marriage . . . it is mainly about displaying the covenant-keeping love between Christ and his church. Knowing Christ is more important than making a living.

John Piper

Love is patient, love is kind. It does not envy, it does not boast, it is not proud. It does not dishonor others, it is not self-seeking, it is not easily angered, it keeps no record of wrongs. Love does not delight in evil but rejoices with the truth. It always protects, always trusts, always hopes, always perseveres.

1 Corinthians 13:4–7

Ian and Larissa began dating while in college. They were filled with hope and anticipation as they planned a future together. A few months before graduation, Ian began shopping for engagement rings. Larissa was confident of his love.

A horrifying car accident on September 30, 2006, altered the course of their lives. A traumatic brain injury left Ian permanently disabled, and it forever changed how they communicated. Larissa moved in with Ian's family to be of help during his difficult rehabilitation and therapy. In spite of the radical change in their future, the couple's love for one another grew.

In Larissa's heart, she cherished all the hopes and wishes of any young woman contemplating marriage and family. She soon realized that her role as a wife would be quite different

177

from her expectations. She would need to work full-time and become a permanent caregiver to her future husband. She also recognized that in spite of Ian's disabilities, his love for God and unwavering trust allowed him to continue to be the spiritual leader of this relationship.

After months of prayer and hours of conversation and tears, Ian and Larissa chose to get married. When describing how they reached this decision, Larissa was straightforward: "It was simple. We love each other. And we love God."[13]

In August of 2010, under shade trees in Western Pennsylvania, Ian and Larissa Murphy made their vows to one another in the presence of family and friends.

As Christian parents and grandparents, we often pray for the person our child or grandchild will marry. We rightfully pray for his or her salvation and character. We pray that this person will have a good job and be responsible. Our list of requests is long. We may even begin to pray for specific abilities or strengths. We pray that our loved ones will marry the right person to make life as secure and uncomplicated as possible.

But . . .

What if God's plan is that our child or grandchild would marry someone who struggles with a disability? Or perhaps someone who has experienced depression or who came from a difficult background? Can God bring this couple joy and satisfaction as they learn to trust Him in these circumstances? Could they, like Ian and Larissa, develop greater faith in God and in each other?

None of these scenarios would be our choice for our child. We would wonder if he or she would be marrying the right person—the person who would fulfill our dreams that together they would live happily ever after.

Of course, it is possible to marry the wrong person. The three A's: abuse, addiction, and adultery plague countless relationships, and the red flags are often evident before the wedding day. Marrying any person in order to save or reform him or her is a prescription for disaster. Walking down the aisle simply to avoid being alone is often a catastrophic choice.

Being the right person is as important as marrying the right person.

Jane came to the suburban Chicago church soon after her gut-wrenching divorce. Her small group consistently prayed for and encouraged the hurting young woman. Frequently, she would lament, "I just married the wrong man."

After one such conversation, my friend Karen blurted out, "Sweetheart, maybe you weren't the right woman."

As we think of our grandchildren's future mates and homes, we can pray that they will say, "I do" to the right person. We pray that they will trust God, follow His leading in a choice of their spouse, be loving and compassionate and true to their vows. We can pray that they will exhibit the characteristics of wisdom, unconditional love, sacrifice, and faith that Ian and Larissa demonstrate in their relationship. We can pray that they will not only *marry* the right person but that they will also *be* the right person.

We can also pray for ourselves. We can pray that we not impose rigid expectations on our grandchild's future husband or wife but learn to be accepting, caring, supportive, and faithful in prayer as they begin their journey toward a mature and Christlike love.

Let Us Pray That . . .

- our grandchildren will understand the permanent nature of the marriage covenant (Matthew 19:4–6).

- our grandchildren will turn to God for wisdom in choosing a spouse (James 1:5).

- our grandchildren avoid relationships that will injure them morally (1 Corinthians 15:33).

- our grandchildren will avoid marrying an angry person (Proverbs 22:24–25).

- our grandchildren will marry a spiritual equal (2 Corinthians 6:14).

- our grandchildren understand that marriage is honorable (Hebrews 13:4).

- our grandchildren grow to understand that marrying someone who fears the Lord will bring the greatest happiness and blessing (Proverbs 31:30).

Heavenly Father, I pray for our grandchildren's marriages. You know how much I love them and how desperately I want each of them to be in a happy and healthy relationship. I pray that they will use wisdom in the choice of the right person for this lifelong relationship. I ask, Father, as my grandchildren begin to date and plan for marriage, that they will be realistic in their expectations and be willing to work hard at loving another person well. It is my prayer that they may not only marry the right person, but will also become the right person with qualities of kindness, patience, and the ability to forgive. May their love for you be their strength and give them the ability to love as you love. I pray that their marriages will reflect the covenant-keeping love between Christ and His church. Amen.

Think and Do

- "The truth is, a successful marriage is not the result of marrying the 'right' person, feeling the 'right' emotions, thinking the 'right' thoughts, or even praying the 'right' prayers. It's about doing the 'right' things—period," says Mark Gungor in his book *Laugh Your Way to a Better Marriage*. What do you agree with in Gungor's quote? What do you disagree with? How can you use these thoughts in your own marriage?

- Are you waiting for your spouse to be the right person? Are there things you should be doing to become the right person?

"So they are no longer two, but one flesh. Therefore what God has joined together, let no one separate" (Matthew 19:6).

"If any of you lacks wisdom, you should ask God, who gives generously to all without finding fault, and it will be given to you" (James 1:5).

"Do not be misled: 'Bad company corrupts good character' " (1 Corinthians 15:33).

"Do not make friends with a hot-tempered person, do not associate with one easily angered, or you may learn their ways and get yourself ensnared" (Proverbs 22:24–25).

"Do not be yoked together with unbelievers. For what do righteousness and wickedness have in common? Or what fellowship can light have with darkness?" (2 Corinthians 6:14).

"Marriage should be honored by all" (Hebrews 13:4).

"Charm is deceptive, and beauty is fleeting; but a woman who fears the LORD is to be praised" (Proverbs 31:30).

day forty-one:
SOUL FOOD

Ordinary riches can be stolen, real riches cannot. In your soul are infinitely precious things that cannot be taken from you.

Oscar Wilde

As the deer pants for streams of water, so my soul pants for you, my God. My soul thirsts for God, for the living God.

Psalm 42:1–2

Only a smidge over five feet tall, Carol was energetic and spry when she was diagnosed with cancer in her seventies. Her doctor encouraged her to undergo a relatively new surgery—something that was unheard of for pancreatic cancer at that time. She agreed. After all, she had gardening to do and volunteer work at the church she loved. She had a husband to care for, children and grandchildren to encourage, and a Monday morning prayer group to attend.

Carol's surgery was successful. When reflecting on her hospital recovery time, she once mentioned to me that the most difficult thing for her was that the nurses kept moving her Bible to a shelf on the other side of the room. When she needed it most, she wanted her well-used Bible close by for comfort. Carol knew that she needed God's Word to feed her soul.

In the story of David at Ziklag, David and his men had lost everything. While off fighting a battle, the entire town had been destroyed. All that remained was a pile of smoking cinders.

The women and children had been hauled away as hostages. Nearly insane with loss and fear, the people wept till they could weep no more.

Exhausted, depleted, and totally overwhelmed, they raged against David—threatening to stone him. David had lost everything—even the respect of his men. Now he faced the prospect of losing his own life. First Samuel records that "David strengthened himself in the LORD his God" (30:6 NKJV).

Some commentaries suggest the verb in that verse hints that David's action of strengthening himself was intentional. He knew where he needed to turn to find the strength to go on. He took responsibility for feeding his own soul by interacting with God and recalling God's help in the past.

I've read that noted twentieth-century theologian Elton Trueblood remarked that we live in a cut-flower civilization. In *Front Porch Tales*, Philip Gulley comments on Trueblood's philosophy: "We sever things from their life source and expect them to flourish. And we cut ourselves off from God and are dismayed when our lives wilt and fade."[14]

Too often, we wait for others to come along and nourish us. We hope that someone else will strengthen us. We blame others for our lack of joy or our stagnant condition. We are starving and thirsty and sit like beggars waiting for crumbs. We cut ourselves off from the very things that would give us peace and joy: worship, study of God's Word, prayer, community, and nature.

Our soul's health and welfare are too important to outsource. The care and feeding of our souls is our own responsibility. Like David, we need to learn to strengthen ourselves in the Lord. Like Carol, we need to keep God's Word close when we need it most.

It is my prayer that my grandchildren will never sever themselves from the true source of life and joy. May they learn how to take responsibility for their own spiritual growth and intentionally strengthen themselves in the Lord.

Let Us Pray That . . .

- our grandchildren grasp how important God's Word is for their lives (Matthew 4:4).

- our grandchildren strengthen themselves with God's Word (Psalm 119:28).
- our grandchildren will be revived by God's Word (Psalm 19:7).
- our grandchildren find joy in God's presence (Psalm 16:11).
- our grandchildren intentionally seek God's face (Psalm 27:8).
- our grandchildren flourish like a tree planted by streams of water as they meditate on God's law (Psalm 1).
- our grandchildren remain in Christ and flourish (John 15:4).
- our grandchildren gain strength as they wait upon the Lord (Isaiah 40:31).

Heavenly Father, forgive me for all the times I have cut myself off from you and the life and peace you offer. Thank you for the example from your Word, which teaches us that we can intentionally strengthen ourselves in you. Lord, I pray that my grandchildren will grasp the concept that they are responsible for coming to you when they are distressed or hurting. May they learn to feed their own souls with your Word and with prayer. I pray that their souls will be fed as they drink in the beauty of your creation. May worship and community fill their hearts and may they be people who flourish like trees planted by streams of water. Amen.

Think and Do

- What is your plan of spiritual self-care? How do you fill your emotional and spiritual tank each day? God's Word? Prayer? Nature? Worship? Solitude? Relationships? Rest? How can you strengthen yourself today and build the inner resilience and faith that life requires?
- Catherine Hart Weber's book on self-care, *Flourish*, reminds us that God has called us to an abundant and joyful life. Could it be that our heavenly Father is pleased when we invest time and energy into our own emotional and spiritual well-being so we can exhibit joy?

- Read the song of David the shepherd boy (Psalm 23), the story of David fighting Goliath (1 Samuel 17), and the story of David at Ziklag (1 Samuel 30:1–6). What habits or characteristics do you notice in David's life that enabled him to be a man after God's own heart? (See 1 Samuel 13:14.)

"Jesus answered, 'It is written: "Man does not live on bread alone, but on every word that comes from the mouth of God" ' " (Matthew 4:4).

"My soul is weary with sorrow; strengthen me according to your word" (Psalm 119:28).

"The law of the LORD is perfect, refreshing the soul. The statutes of the LORD are trustworthy, making wise the simple" (Psalm 19:7).

"You make known to me the path of life; you fill me with joy in your presence, with eternal pleasures at your right hand" (Psalm 16:11).

"My heart says of you, 'Seek his face!' Your face, LORD, I will seek" (Psalm 27:8).

"Blessed is the one who does not walk in step with the wicked or stand in the way that sinners take or sit in the company of mockers, but whose delight is in the law of the LORD, and who meditates on his law day and night. That person is like a tree planted by streams of water, which yields its fruit in season and whose leaf does not wither—whatever they do prospers" (Psalm 1:1–3).

"Remain in me, as I also remain in you" (John 15:4).

"But those who hope in the LORD will renew their strength" (Isaiah 40:31).

day forty-two:
PENNY CANDY

Never does the human soul appear so strong and noble as when it foregoes revenge and dares to forgive injury.

Edward Hubble Chapin

Be kind and compassionate to one another, forgiving each other, just as in Christ God forgave you.

Ephesians 4:32

My father passed away on Good Friday. His funeral was the following Tuesday.

Dad came from a large Irish family of seven. Years of conflict had shattered my father's family and left my sisters and me confused. We loved our grandparents, our aunt, uncles, and cousins. For years, we felt the loss of them in our lives. In spite of the family turmoil, Uncle Vernon and Aunt Jeanie kept the door ajar, and we communicated with them from time to time.

We were honored to see them at my father's funeral. Aunt Jeanie was as beautiful, kind, and fun-loving as ever. Uncle Vernon had changed little in forty years. I remembered him as a dark-haired, blue-eyed Irish boy who was Cary Grant handsome. Before the family conflict, when our family still visited my dad's boyhood home for Sunday dinners, Uncle Vernon greeted his little nieces with laughter and teasing.

While Grandma mashed potatoes in the kitchen, Uncle Vernon would pick me up, swing me around, and put me down in the middle of Grandma's perfectly polished dining room table.

"Mother! Mother!" Uncle Vernon would yell, "Kay is dancing on the table again!" Shaking her mashed potato laden spoon, my four-foot-ten grandmother would charge through the doorway chiding, "Get down from there, young lady. Vernon, stop teasing her right now!"

In a panic, I scampered down from the table. In less than five minutes I found myself, once again, in the middle of Grandma's table.

After my father's funeral service, the family gathered in my mother's Tennessee home for ham sandwiches. Our still charming and handsome uncle told stories about my father.

My dad, Thomas, was the oldest child in this Depression-era family. He was also the oldest child in the Irish Catholic neighborhood. His age and role as the firstborn put him in a position of responsibility for the younger kids. He was given the job of walking neighbor children to the Catholic school not far away. After school, he would escort them home before going to a part-time job sweeping sidewalks in front of a local hardware store. All week, he would save the few cents he earned.

On Fridays, Tom would fill his pockets with the precious pennies. After school, this freckle-faced boy would pass out coins to the children as he led them home by way of the candy store.

Seeing Uncle Vernon again brought back tender memories. I recalled a nativity set in my grandmother's living room. During the Depression, Christmas decorations were a luxury no one could afford. My father had rescued a discarded sewing machine case that he then fashioned into the stable. With pieces of this and bits of that and a whole lot of cotton batting, he filled the stable with Mary, Joseph, Baby Jesus, and assorted animals. As long as my grandmother remained in her home, the handmade nativity set was placed by the fireplace each Christmas.

Young Thomas had a kind, generous, and creative heart.

Sadly, my father's life didn't continue on the same path. I have often asked myself what changed a generous and creative young man into such an unhappy and often surly person. That is a question that will never be answered.

But the lesson of penny candy spoke to me. Behind every sad life is usually a sad story—a story of tragedy or hurt or betrayal or abandonment or rejection from which the person has never recovered. I am sure this was the case with my father.

Dr. Everett Worthington has created an acronym for the process of forgiveness: REACH. The E in the acronym stands for *empathy*.[15] Over the years, Dr. Worthington has discovered that it is impossible to fully forgive someone until we experience some degree of compassion for that person. When someone has hurt us, the last thing we want to do is feel kindness for him or her. But empathy is essential for forgiveness.

I want to learn to be compassionate toward those who have hurt me. I want to have a tender heart and be able to sincerely empathize. I am not there yet, but Uncle Vernon's story of penny candy has moved me one step closer.

I pray that my grandchildren will look beyond a person's actions and words to have compassion for the person who has hurt them. I pray that they will REACH a place where they can pray, do good, and bless those who harm them.

Let Us Pray That . . .

- our grandchildren mature into lovers of mercy (Micah 6:8).
- our grandchildren understand the limitless forgiveness of God (Luke 17:4).
- our grandchildren totally embrace the lesson Jesus communicated in the parable of the unmerciful servant (Matthew 18:23–35).
- our grandchildren will have compassion on those who have strayed from God (Matthew 9:36).
- our grandchildren learn to pray for those who hurt them (Matthew 5:44).
- our grandchildren resist the temptation to judge and condemn those who have hurt them (Luke 6:46).

Heavenly Father, it is so easy for me to condemn others before I give a thought to the pain lodged in their hearts. May I study Jesus and how truthful and merciful He was at all times. You have forgiven me so much; please keep me from becoming the unmerciful servant who was unable to forgive. I pray for the people who have hurt me and ask that you would bind up their wounds. I pray for the people I have hurt, that they would extend their forgiveness to me. I pray for my grandchildren, who will inevitably face hurts and injuries. May they be quick to forgive and wise enough to hold others accountable. May they know when to put up boundaries to prevent further damage. Blend together in their lives that mixture of truth and grace that came with Jesus. The world is filled with hurting people who go on to hurt others. Lord Jesus, come and heal all our wounds. Amen.

Think and Do

- Matthew 5:44 tells us how to respond to those who have hurt us. We are to pray for them, do good to them, and bless them. The word for *bless* means "speak well." Have your grandchildren heard you speak well of someone who has harmed you? What good characteristic about that person have you noted and could mention? Have they heard you pray for that person? When that person faces misfortune, are you the first there with a casserole, plate of cookies, or word of comfort?

- Pearl S. Buck's book *The Big Wave* tells the story of Kino and Jiya in Japan. After a tsunami and the loss of his family, Jiya is embraced by Kino's family and allowed to grieve at his own rate and to eventually recover. The tenderness of this family is a beautiful picture of how God might use us to bring healing to a hurting person. This is a great read-aloud book.

- Dr. Henry Cloud and Dr. John Townsend have done wonderful work on boundaries. Forgiving someone is not the same as allowing them to continually cause you pain. Choose one of the Cloud-Townsend *Boundaries* books to learn how to be a forgiving person who establishes appropriate boundaries.

- Do you have past hurts that affect your relationships with family and friends? Do you find yourself saying and doing things you regret? There is healing for your hurts. Find a trusted counselor in your area and allow someone to care for you as you move forward in a process of healing. Give it time.

"He has showed you, O mortal, what is good. And what does the LORD require of you? To act justly and to love mercy and to walk humbly with your God" (Micah 6:8).

"If your brother or sister sins against you, rebuke them; and if they repent, forgive them. Even if they sin against you seven times in a day and seven times come back to you saying, 'I repent,' you must forgive them" (Luke 17:3–4).

"Shouldn't you have had mercy on your fellow servant just as I had on you?" (Matthew 18:33).

"When he saw the crowds, he had compassion on them, because they were harassed and helpless, like sheep without a shepherd" (Matthew 9:36).

"But I tell you, love your enemies and pray for those who persecute you, that you may be children of your Father in heaven" (Matthew 5:44–45).

"Do not judge, and you will not be judged. Do not condemn, and you will not be condemned. Forgive, and you will be forgiven" (Luke 6:37).

day forty-three:
BAREFOOT HOPE

Hope is a waking dream.

Augustine

May the God of hope fill you with all joy and peace as you trust in him, so that you may overflow with hope by the power of the Holy Spirit.

Romans 15:13

It was a blustery day. Yet the mild March temperatures enticed our ginger-haired, four-year-old granddaughter to explore the muddy backyard. Looking out the kitchen window, I was surprised to see her taking off her shoes and flinging her socks in the air. Barefoot and dancing for joy, she asked, "Grandma, where is my pool? Can Papa put up the swing? Summer is here."

"No, Nikki. Summer isn't here. It is too cold for your pool. You need to put your shoes and socks back on!"

"But Grandma, look at the trees! Summer is here." Specks of green dotted the branches of the maple tree as new buds formed. Each bud was a promise of the summer to come.

How easily she observed this subtle message of nature. For our dancing, gleeful little girl, spying the buds on the trees made it as good as summer. She was filled with hope. Barefoot hope—a hope that made her act in faith on the promise of warmth, sunshine, and hours on a swing.

In Matthew 24, Jesus told the parable of the fig tree. "Now learn this parable from the fig tree: As soon as its twigs get tender and its leaves come out, you know that summer is near" (v. 32). He shared this parable to encourage His followers to be as observant about watching for the signs of His coming as they were about anticipating the coming of summer.

I hope for His coming. But it generally isn't a barefoot hope—not a hope that makes me act as if His coming is near. It is more of a "wouldn't it be nice" hope that does little to change my daily life.

I need to become as observant and excited about the signs of His coming as Nikki was about the coming of summer.

I want my grandchildren to have barefoot hope. Hope in His promises. Hope in their future. Hope that God will always be with them, even in their struggles. Hope for forgiveness. Hope for divine intervention. Hope for healing of hurts and broken relationships. Hope that Jesus is coming again to right the wrongs of this world and to take us to live with Him.

Romans 15:13 gives a simple prescription for being filled with hope. "May the God of hope fill you with all joy and peace as you trust in him, so that you may overflow with hope by the power of the Holy Spirit."

We trust. God fills. We overflow.

I pray that my grandchildren will trust God and His promises. I pray that as they trust they will overflow with a barefoot hope that makes them sing and dance for joy.

Now, everyone take off your shoes!

Let Us Pray That . . .

- our grandchildren hope in Christ all the day long (Psalm 25:5).

- our grandchildren know that their hope is in Christ alone (Psalm 39:7).

- our grandchildren find strength as they hope in the Lord (Isaiah 40:31).

- our grandchildren will hope in the Lord from their youth (Psalm 71:5).

- our grandchildren experience the hope that does not disappoint (Romans 5:5).
- our grandchildren's hope in Christ will make them bold (2 Corinthians 3:12).
- our grandchildren have a living hope (1 Peter 1:3).
- our grandchildren hope for His coming (Titus 2:13).

Heavenly Father, I thank you for the joyful hope I have seen in my granddaughter. Please preserve that spirit of hope within her. Lord, I want to dance for joy as I think of your promises. I ask that you would help my grandchildren to trust in you and in your promises so they will overflow with joy and hope. When they feel hopeless, may they turn to your Word and find reason to have faith again. Remind them of your love and care. Father, help us all to trust you so you can fill us to overflowing with hope. Amen.

Think and Do

- Create a hope chest for your grandchildren. Fill it with stories about their baby days, photos, Bible verses, and little gifts. Leave each child a letter about your hope for his or her future.
- Read *Here Comes Summer* by Mary Murphy with your preschool and early elementary grandchildren. Be on the outlook for signs of changing seasons. With great anticipation, watch for the signs of Christ's return.
- Do you need hope for a difficult time? Nancy Guthrie's *The One Year Book of Hope* will give you 365 days of readings that will encourage you to trust in God's care.

"Guide me in your truth and teach me, for you are God my Savior, and my hope is in you all day long" (Psalm 25:5).

"But now, Lord, what do I look for? My hope is in you" (Psalm 39:7).

"But those who hope in the LORD will renew their strength. They will soar on wings like eagles; they will run and not grow weary, they will walk and not be faint" (Isaiah 40:31).

"And hope does not put us to shame, because God's love has been poured into our hearts through the Holy Spirit, who has been given to us" (Romans 5:5).

"Therefore, since we have such a hope, we are very bold" (2 Corinthians 3:12).

"For you have been my hope, Sovereign LORD, my confidence since my youth" (Psalm 71:5).

"Praise be to the God and Father of our Lord Jesus Christ! In his great mercy he has given us new birth into a living hope through the resurrection of Jesus Christ from the dead, and into an inheritance that can never perish, spoil or fade. This inheritance is kept in heaven for you" (1 Peter 1:3–4).

"We wait for the blessed hope—the appearing of the glory of our great God and Savior, Jesus Christ" (Titus 2:13).

day forty-four:
BREAKFAST IN BED

Perfectionism becomes the badge of honor with you playing the suffering hero.

David Burns

Surely there is not a righteous man on earth who does good and never sins.

Ecclesiastes 7:20 ESV

Chattering children, clanging pans, and the smell of burnt toast reminded me it was Saturday morning. Cozy under the comforter in my sunny bedroom, I listened to our four children arguing in the kitchen. I was going to be honored with breakfast in bed.

Soon, the four—still in footed pajamas—knocked on my door. With big smiles, they presented me with a wobbling tray of food and shouts of "Mommy! We made you breakfast in bed!"

Laughing and pleased with themselves for offering this gift to me, they clambered into bed to watch and bounce as I enjoyed the watery scrambled eggs, lukewarm orange juice, weak tea, and burnt toast. It was one of the most delightful breakfasts I have ever eaten. I finished every last forkful.

Satisfied with their gift and with my reaction, they snuggled under the blankets and we read a book or two. My children had full and giving hearts. I was a blessed woman.

Was it a gourmet meal? No. A well-executed omelet? Not at all. Fit for the Food Network? Nope. Was it prepared and offered in love? Absolutely.

Perfection was unnecessary.

As parents and grandparents, we never reject a child's hand drawing of our family, a tree, or a dog. We *ooh* and *aah* and hang it on the fridge. We never spurn a fistful of dandelions from a toddler. We reach for the best vase and set it in the middle of the dining room table—then turn and give the little one a kiss.

The best gifts presented to us are not perfect or expensive or elaborate. We prize the gifts given from a heart of love. These presents do exactly what the giver intends. They touch our hearts. They communicate honor and importance. They melt our hearts and leave an enduring memory.

Psychologists and counselors are aware that we all think, feel, and act out life based on our core beliefs. For some, the driving core belief is that everything I do must be perfect or I am not a worthwhile and valuable person. If it is not completely perfect, I am a failure and unworthy of love. If I am not perfect, I will be rejected. I must be perfect. I must be perfect. I must be perfect.

Could perfectionism be about fear? Anne Lamott writes, "Perfectionism is the voice of the oppressor." Individuals seeking perfection in themselves and others suffer gut-wrenching oppression as they live daily in fear of failure and ultimately of rejection.

Perfectionists have a sense of security and relief as they pull off blissful moments of faultlessness. It never lasts. Unable to keep up the appearance of perfection, they slide into despair the moment they are aware of their human flaws and limitations.

The quest for perfection kills authenticity. Hiding who we are is the only way we can deal with our blemishes. It sets young people up for eating disorders as they try to replicate the image of perfection that is in their heads. It wreaks havoc on relationships as the demands on each person increase. Love is lost.

Oh, the misery of not being able to offer simple imperfect gifts from a heart of love to the people and God we adore. Oh, the agony of needing to be perfect.

Self-righteous Pharisees were careful to follow the law to the tiniest detail. It comforted them and gave them a false sense of security as they congratulated themselves on tithing from their paltry spices.

Shaking them from their smugness, Jesus warned them, "Woe to you, teachers of the law and Pharisees, you hypocrites! You give a tenth of your spices—mint, dill and cumin. But you have neglected the more important matters of the law—justice, mercy and faithfulness. You should have practiced the latter, without neglecting the former" (Matthew 23:23).

It is possible to get so mired in the details of doing things perfectly that we lose sight of the weightier issues of life: justice and mercy and faithfulness.

God knows I am not perfect. I know I am not perfect. Our relationship only requires that He be perfect and that I be His child. To this date, God has never snubbed me when I have approached Him while carrying a wobbly tray of imperfect works that were done out of a heart filled with love.

He swings open the door and receives my gifts as any truly loving Father would. I love Him for that.

I pray that my grandchildren will not fall prey to the secular and sometimes Christian false belief of perfectionism. I pray that they will be able to serve God with hearts full of love, free from fear, and confident of His welcome.

Let Us Pray That . . .

- our grandchildren realize that acceptance is not based on performance but on the mercy of God (Romans 5:8).

- our grandchildren understand that Jesus never turns away those who wholeheartedly come to Him (John 6:37).

- our grandchildren understand that God's grace is sufficient in weakness (2 Corinthians 12:9–10).

- our grandchildren know that God alone is perfect (2 Samuel 22:31).

- our grandchildren accept that no one will ever attain perfection in this life but will continue on in following the Lord (Philippians 3:12).

- our grandchildren will not try to attain perfection through human effort (Galatians 3:3).

- our grandchildren acknowledge that everything they need for life and godliness has been given to them through God's divine power—not through human effort (2 Peter 1:3).

Heavenly Father, your grace is sufficient for my weakness. My desire for perfection is fulfilled in you, for you are the only one who is perfect in all of your ways. Grant me the humility to realize that I will never reach perfection in this life. I pray that my grandchildren will reject the culture's call to be perfect on their jobs, in their parenting, in their marriages, in their appearance, and in their faith. Allow them to release others from unrealistic expectations. Lord, teach them to avoid hiding themselves and their flaws but to be authentic in their relationship with family, friends, and you. May they know the simple joy of being the child of a loving and caring heavenly Father, who never rejects those who come to Him with open hearts. We love you, Lord, and we pray that you will help us to attend to the weightier matters of life: justice, mercy, and faithfulness. Amen.

Think and Do

- The media and entertainment worlds hurl messages at young people about the need to be perfect. These messages are damaging and oppressive. What do you notice in media that could be setting a trap for your grandchildren? What brief word of wisdom can you share with them? Can you finish this sentence? "God does not ask us to be perfect. He asks us to . . ."

- Do you have a grandchild who is determined to do everything perfectly? *Ish* by Peter Reynolds tells the story of Ramon. Ramon loved to draw but was discouraged because his drawing of a vase didn't look like a vase. His sister helped him to understand that if his drawing looked vase-ish that was good enough. Kids will learn that you don't have to draw, sing, dance, or do any activity perfectly in order to enjoy it.

"But God demonstrates his own love for us in this: While we were still sinners, Christ died for us" (Romans 5:8).

"All those the Father gives me will come to me, and whoever comes to me I will never drive away" (John 6:37).

"But he said to me, 'My grace is sufficient for you, for my power is made perfect in weakness.' Therefore I will boast all the more gladly about my weaknesses, so that Christ's power may rest on me" (2 Corinthians 12:9).

"As for God, his way is perfect: The LORD's word is flawless; he shields all who take refuge in him" (2 Samuel 22:31).

"Not that I have already obtained all this, or have already arrived at my goal, but I press on to take hold of that for which Christ Jesus took hold of me" (Philippians 3:12).

"Are you so foolish? After beginning by means of the Spirit, are you now trying to finish by means of the flesh?" (Galatians 3:3).

"His divine power has given us everything we need for a godly life through our knowledge of him who called us by his own glory and goodness" (2 Peter 1:3).

day forty-five:
WALTER AND DOROTHY

You can see God from anywhere if your mind is set to love and obey Him.

A. W. Tozer

True worshipers will worship the Father in the Spirit and in truth, for they are the kind of worshipers the Father seeks.

John 4:23

Walter ran. When the cold rain raged and soaked him to the skin, he ran. When snow swirled and ice stung his face, he ran. When heat and Midwest humidity drained him of strength, he ran. With dedication and determination, day after day, Walter laced up his shoes and repeatedly sprinted up and down the hill in a local landfill. The slope was so steep and treacherous that if Walter had rested from the grueling climb for even a second, he would slide to the bottom. He couldn't stop.

Walter Payton's hill is now part of Nickol Knoll Golf Club in Arlington Heights, Illinois. Once an important part of his extreme training, today the hill is marked by a plaque honoring one of the NFL's finest running backs and one of Chicago's most beloved citizens.

Gary, a friend and gifted musician, explained to me that Walter ran so he would be prepared to do his job on the football field in any kind of weather. His training prepared him to adapt to every situation. Gary also remarked that Christians should be equally dedicated and intent as they train themselves to worship God in any circumstance.

The Samaritan woman brought this question to Jesus. Where should she worship? On this hill or in Jerusalem? She mistakenly believed that worship was about form and location. Jesus instructed, "true worshipers will worship . . . in the Spirit and in truth, for they are the kind of worshipers the Father seeks" (John 4:23). Jesus made it clear that worship is about having hearts that are prepared for authentic, truth-filled worship. When that is true, we can worship anywhere.

We go into training for many things. Some train to run marathons. Others train for races or tournaments. On-the-job training helps people improve their skills and provides new opportunities. Professional athletes train every day. Serious musicians practice for hours.

Writing to Timothy, Paul says that we should train ourselves to be godly: "For physical training is of some value, but godliness has value in all things, holding promise for both the present life and the life to come" (1 Timothy 4:8).

Dorothy Wright has spent nine decades training for godliness. Dorothy and her husband, Phil, were active church members all of their lives. They opened their home to pastors and missionaries. When our family returned home from three years in France, the Wrights moved out of their house into a basement apartment in the home of a family member so our family would have a familiar place to live. Our children loved that home.

Phil and Dorothy supported missionaries around the world. There is no way to know the full impact of their sacrifice and generosity.

This couple had a daily routine of Bible reading and prayer that nothing could disrupt. They were as diligent in their spiritual disciplines as Walter Payton was in his athletic training. They prayed when life was good. They prayed when life was a struggle. They prayed when friends suffered. They praised when there was reason to rejoice. Their devotion to intercessory prayer was an important part of our lives. Dorothy prayed for our children almost daily during our years as missionaries.

Not long ago, Phil passed away. In her mid-nineties, Dorothy now lives with her son and daughter-in-law. In spite of her age, health difficulties, and recent loss, Dorothy has not allowed her routine of spiritual disciplines to miss a beat. Her daughter-in-law, Becky, told me, "I have lived with Dorothy for ten years now and have been impressed with her continued need to be in the Word and in fellowship with God. She remains vital as a prayer warrior."

I am not as trained in worship and prayer as I could be. My daily habits have not been as consistent as either Walter's or Dorothy's. It isn't too late.

My prayer is that my grandchildren's generation will renew a spirit of devotion to Jesus and will develop consistent daily habits of engaging in spiritual disciplines. I pray that they will be so thoroughly trained in personal worship and prayer that they will be able to worship God in all circumstances.

Let Us Pray That . . .

- our grandchildren worship God in spirit and in truth (John 4:24).
- our grandchildren will be part of a generation that trains for godliness (1 Timothy 4:8).
- our grandchildren embrace Scripture for training in godliness (2 Timothy 3:16).
- our grandchildren experience the joy of meeting with God each day (Psalm 5:3).
- our grandchildren cultivate a life of prayer (Ephesians 6:18).
- our grandchildren accept the cultural differences in worship styles as a reflection of God's great plan for humanity (Revelation 7:9).
- our grandchildren participate in community and corporate worship (Hebrews 10:25).

Heavenly Father, forgive me for being negligent in my own training in personal holiness and devotion. Renew in my generation a passion for your Word and prayer. Allow us the honor and privilege of modeling to our grandchildren a life marked by spiritual discipline. We pray that our grandchildren will learn early the habits of daily Bible reading, prayer, and worship. May they approach their own spiritual formation with the same dedication and energy that they give to all other areas of life. Lord, we know you are seeking worshipers who will worship you with all of their hearts. We ask, Father, that our grandchildren will be those worshipers. May they be so trained in personal worship that they can enter any sanctuary around the world and be able to join in heartfelt corporate worship with your people. Amen.

Think and Do

- Many years ago, my husband visited churches in Port-au-Prince, Haiti. One evening, he drove with a pastor into the hills outside of the city to attend a youth worship service. Partway through the service, the electricity went out. The young people, totally in the dark, continued to sing and worship. It was one of the most moving worship experiences of his life. These teens were able to worship in a difficult circumstance. Have you had a similar experience? Can you share that with your grandchild?

- Philippians 2:3 tells us to "Do nothing out of selfish ambition or vain conceit. Rather, in humility value others above yourselves." Sometimes, our personal preferences get in the way of our worship experience. How can this verse help in this situation? How can you train yourself to participate in worship even when the style is unfamiliar?

- Daniel was carried away from his home and country. Yet his spiritual training went with him to Babylon. Read your grandchildren the story of Daniel, and discuss the ways he was trained to love and serve God at all times. Connie Neal's book *Walking Tall in Babylon* has helpful thoughts for parents and grandparents who want children to have the spiritual strength of a Daniel.

"God is spirit, and his worshipers must worship in the Spirit and in truth" (John 4:24).

"All Scripture is God-breathed and is useful for teaching, rebuking, correcting and training in righteousness" (2 Timothy 3:16).

"In the morning, LORD, you hear my voice; in the morning I lay my requests before you and wait expectantly" (Psalm 5:3).

"And pray in the Spirit on all occasions with all kinds of prayers and requests. With this in mind, be alert and always keep on praying for all the LORD's people" (Ephesians 6:18).

"After this I looked, and there before me was a great multitude that no one could count, from every nation, tribe, people and language, standing before the throne and before the Lamb. They were wearing white robes and were holding palm branches in their hands" (Revelation 7:9).

"Not giving up meeting together, as some are in the habit of doing, but encouraging one another—and all the more as you see the Day approaching" (Hebrews 10:25).

"For physical training is of some value, but godliness has value for all things, holding promise for both the present life and the life to come" (1 Timothy 4:8).

day forty-six:
A BLACK AND WHITE WORLD

I am thoroughly convinced the Christian faith is the most coherent worldview around.

Ravi Zacharias

Lift up your hands to him for the lives of your children.

Lamentations 2:19

"Grandma, what was the world like when everything was black and white?"

After Kevin had watched a few *Leave It to Beaver* episodes with his mom, his busy brain concluded that what he saw on television proved that the world was colorless till the 1970s.

My feeble attempts to explain the technology only frustrated him. What he actually wanted to know was what the world was like when I was a girl.

This is what I told him: "I remember spending hours outside. My sisters and I walked to a small convenience store for ice cream. We took strolls down a shady country road to nowhere with our friends. We hiked to a creek or through the woods without a worry. There were few after-school activities in those days. We were free to spend hours on the rope swing in the backyard or lie in the grass under the maple tree.

"Most moms were home and watched over all the neighborhood kids. We felt safe and had enormous freedom.

"Summers were precious. They seemed to go on forever. We designed our own imaginary worlds and played for hours.

Even girls played cops and robbers. Most families didn't have air conditioning, but no one cared. A hose or sprinkler or inflatable pool did nicely. The Ohio Valley humidity gave us a good excuse to lie in the grass to read a book. I must have read *Little Women* ten times. Summer evenings, Grandma sat on the front porch telling us stories of her own childhood while we watched for lightning bugs. Sometimes, *Monopoly* was the passion. We could keep a game going for a week.

"We didn't watch much television. If we did, it was *The Wonderful World of Disney* or *The Mickey Mouse Club*. Romantic movies were silly and sweet. After weeks of chasing the girl, the young man finally got his long-awaited kiss as the movie ended.

"I loved school. I wasn't a great student, but I remember some important moments. We began each morning with the 'Pledge of Allegiance' and then heard a short prayer broadcast over the intercom. At the end of the ritual Friday pep rally we recited the Lord's Prayer in unison. It is hard to believe those things were accepted as normal.

"No shopping on Sundays. Even families that didn't go to church rested. My sisters and I spread the comics out on the living room floor while our mother cooked a pot roast or chicken legs and mashed potatoes. Sunday was often game day. Grandma was a *Scrabble* genius. I never won.

"Christians were respected and free to share their faith. Our neighbors, the Johnsons, would take us to church and prayed for us. They were my first spiritual parents.

"We knew that it was wrong to lie, cheat, or hurt another person. We were taught to respect our elders, admire people of faith, and be kind. But what I remember most about my childhood is that we played and played and played."

I loved Kevin's response after I shared a few of these thoughts with him. "Grandma, I wish I had lived then."

"Me too, Kevin. Me too."

I hold no illusions that we baby boomers grew up in a perfect world. For our parents, World War II was a recent memory. Millions of young fathers were suffering from what we now call post-traumatic stress disorder (PTSD). The resources for families to deal with stress, trauma, financial issues, and marriage problems did not exist. Many suffered in silence. Children were left comfortless. Neighbors turned a blind eye to domestic violence. College educations were available to only a few. Many fathers worked more than one job to put food on the table. As always, children struggled with rebellious behavior, and husbands and wives argued. Alcohol abuse grew, and treatment for addiction was limited. Sadly, millions of American citizens were unable to participate fully in the rights and privileges of our society. Many injustices still needed correcting. Life was far from perfect.

However, in the 1960s and 1970s the move to secularize our culture went into full swing. Freedom from moral restraints became the war cry, and this triumphed in the 1973 Supreme Court *Roe v. Wade* decision. Abortion scarred our national soul. Premarital sex was now encouraged and applauded. Moral and values education shifted from the home and church to the school while at the same time the Christian worldview was booted out of our educational system. Divorce statistics rose along with drug and alcohol addiction.

While the 1950s were not the good old days that we imagine, there was an implied moral code that made life easier for young people and at the very least encouraged the integrity of the family unit.

Perhaps, in my time, it truly was more of a black-and-white world.

I am not praying that we will go back to those days. Reciting the Lord's Prayer at the end of a pep rally does little to insure that a young person will embrace a vibrant faith. Having Sundays free was relaxing but didn't result in spiritual growth.

This is my prayer: May the eyes of the grandparents of our generation be opened to the tremendous challenges faced by our grandchildren, and may we devote ourselves to prayer.

This call to prayer is serious business.

The sexual freedom endorsed by our culture, the ease of obtaining drugs of every kind, the pervasive messages of the media and the explicit nature of entertainment, the crudeness of the national language, the cheapness of human life, the false spirituality that is so widely accepted, and the marginalization of the Christian worldview in favor of secular humanism are things that we did not face.

If there has ever been a time when a generation needed a visit from God, it is now.

Let Us Pray That . . .

- our grandchildren have the courage of Daniel (Daniel 6:11).
- our grandchildren have the integrity of Joseph (Genesis 39:10).
- our grandchildren have boldness of Esther (Esther 4:14; 7:3).
- our grandchildren have the heart of David (Acts 13:22).
- our grandchildren have the clear message of the gospel like Paul (Romans 1:16).
- we will reject anxiety in favor of prayer (Philippians 4:6).
- we will understand that whatever good comes from our prayer it is all because of God's great mercy (Daniel 9:18).
- we will pray as long as it takes (Luke 18:1).

Heavenly Father, you know how our hearts ache for our children and grandchildren as they face so many challenges. We long for them to have a simpler life that will nurture them emotionally and spiritually. Most of all, we long for them to have a Christian worldview that will give them hope and courage in the face of opposition. Father, help us to be skilled in our own apologetics and to be ready to give our grandchildren an answer for the hope that is within us. Lord, you promised that you would send another Advocate to us that would teach us all things. Thank you for fulfilling your promise and sending your Holy Spirit. We pray, Father, that your Holy Spirit would teach our grandchildren the truth and fill them with your power. Lord, we refuse to despair. Rather, we hope in you all day long. Amen.

Think and Do

- It is easy for us to criticize what we see in the next generation without considering the cultural changes over which they had no control. Are there sins our generation needs to confess before revival can come (Proverbs 28:13)?

- It is difficult to clearly articulate a Christian worldview. Will you accept the challenge? The writings of C. S. Lewis, Francis Schaeffer, Lee Strobel, and Ravi Zacharias can help you hone your skills in sharing your faith.

- Daniel, Joseph, Esther, and David were still young when God used them. Frequently, revivals begin with a younger generation. How can we encourage the next generation of young Christian leaders (Titus 2:6–8)?

- Consider starting a grandparents' prayer group in your church or neighborhood. Share not only your concerns but also your hopes.

"Then these men went as a group and found Daniel praying and asking God for help" (Daniel 6:11).

"And though she spoke to Joseph day after day, he refused to go to bed with her or even be with her" (Genesis 39:10).

"And who knows but that you have come to your royal position for such a time as this?" (Esther 4:14).

"After removing Saul, he made David their king. God testified concerning him: 'I have found David son of Jesse, a man after my own heart; he will do everything I want him to do' " (Acts 13:22).

"For I am not ashamed of the gospel, because it is the power of God that brings salvation to everyone who believes: first to the Jew, then to the Gentile" (Romans 1:16).

"Do not be anxious about anything, but in every situation, by prayer and petition, with thanksgiving, present your requests to God" (Philippians 4:6).

"Then Jesus told his disciples a parable to show them that they should always pray and not give up" (Luke 18:1).

day forty-seven:
GLUED TO JESUS

Never hold on to anything tighter than you hold on to God.
Linda Evans Shepherd

I cling to you; your right hand upholds me.
Psalm 63:8

Sucked under the churning water for nearly three minutes, Maria reached out into the swirling, debris-filled darkness for something solid to take hold of. When she finally surfaced, gasping for air, she wrapped her battered arms around a half-submerged tree. Screaming at the horrific sight of devastation in front of her, she reached an obvious conclusion. Her family was gone.

Then, in the distance, she saw her oldest son, Lucas, struggling against the raging water. Alternately being pulled under and then bobbing to the surface, he would hear his mother shout above the roar for him to grab on to something! Miraculously, exhausted and terrified, they worked their way toward each other, and mother and son both found something to hold on to. They found each other.

For Maria and Lucas Belons, whose story was depicted in the movie *The Impossible*, clinging to one another during the Boxing Day Tsunami of 2004 saved both of their lives.

What we cling to in life has the potential to save us or to bring us heartache. In Psalm 63, David writes of his great desire for and delight in God. Finding his deepest satisfaction in God, he proclaims, "I cling to you; your right hand upholds me" (v. 8). The Hebrew word for *cling* means to "adhere to." The word for *glue* is derived from the same word. David is attaching his very heart and soul to God.

The world offers us a variety of things to which we can cling. We can cling to money as a source of security. It can never save us. We can cling to success or our professions. Eventually, success becomes meaningless. Sometimes we glue ourselves to unhealthy relationships because we just don't want to be alone. We cling to appearances, wanting to look flawless in the eyes of others. We bond our hearts to popularity or fame. All of these things are flimsy and temporary, and they never keep us afloat for long.

Clinging to God never disappoints. Wrapping our hearts around Him brings peace and satisfaction. Riveting our hearts to Jesus brings true security. Holding fast to the Lord helps us to survive the storms of life.

Nearly forty years ago, I heard a college professor share the same verse from Psalm 63. He used the illustration of a vine wrapped around a tree. "Eventually," he said, "the tree and the vine grow together until you don't know where one starts and the other ends."

Could it be true that the tighter we cling to Jesus the more like Him we become?

I know that life will bring storms for my grandchildren. They will occasionally be sucked under by the current of life. When they resurface, they will need something—no, they will need Someone—to cling to. I pray that they will not cling to the things of this world that are so fleeting. My prayer is that they will cling so tightly to Jesus that over the years they will look more and more like Him.

Let Us Pray That . . .

- our grandchildren trust in Jesus in the difficult times (John 14:1).
- our grandchildren will not lose their courage but will hold fast and persevere (Hebrews 10:35–36).

- our grandchildren hold fast to the Lord as Joshua commanded the people (Joshua 23:8).

- our grandchildren hold solidly to their hope in Jesus Christ (Hebrews 10:23).

Heavenly Father, in this ever-changing world, our children and grandchildren are looking for something solid and sure to cling to. Forgive us, Lord, for the times we have thought that holding fast to success or money would bring us satisfaction and security. Help us to learn how to truly embrace you and to wrap our affection and trust around only you. We pray that we can become examples to our children and grandchildren. As we cling to Jesus, make us more like Him. Help us to point our children and grandchildren to you as the only One they need to cling to. May they cling to you more and more as the years go by. May they grow to be like Jesus. Amen.

Think and Do

- Read Romans 12:9. Paul instructed the people of Rome to "hate what is evil; cling to what is good." What does that mean for our day?

- Second Thessalonians 2:15 also tells us to hold fast to the teachings we have received. Think about ways you can renew your commitment to the things you are learning from God's Word and to growing closer to Him.

- Using Psalm 63:8, do an art project with your grandkids. Cut hearts of various colors and sizes and put one word from the verse on each heart. Allow the kids to glue their hearts to a larger sheet of paper so they "write out" the entire verse. As they glue, teach them that *cling* can also mean "to glue." Talk to them about ways you are "gluing" your own heart to Jesus. Take time to pray a prayer of blessing for each child.

"Do not let your hearts be troubled. You believe in God; believe also in me" (John 14:1).

"So do not throw away your confidence; it will be richly rewarded. You need to persevere so that when you have done the will of God, you will receive what he has promised" (Hebrews 10:35–36).

"But you are to hold fast to the LORD your God, as you have until now" (Joshua 23:8).

"Let us hold unswervingly to the hope we profess, for he who promised is faithful" (Hebrews 10:23).

day forty-eight:
MARVELOUS LIGHT

The issue is now clear. It is between light and darkness and everyone must choose his side.

G. K. Chesterton

When Jesus spoke again to the people, he said, "I am the light of the world. Whoever follows me will never walk in darkness, but will have the light of life."

John 8:12

Light. It does so many things.

As medical lasers, light heals. Light is used to irradiate food and water—making these necessities of life safe. Light brings warmth. It transforms frozen winter earth into life-producing soil for tulips and daffodils. Plant life depends on light for the chemical reaction of photosynthesis. Light from our superheated sun races to the earth in eight minutes.

Without the energy-producing light of the sun, life would be impossible.

In the winter, when we receive less warmth from our sun because of the tilt of the earth, we treasure every hour of sunlight and rejoice as each day grows longer. The light from a fireplace illuminates and chases away the chill of a fall night and creates a cozy atmosphere to gather with family and friends.

Light illuminates, allowing us to go about our daily routines. Man-made light enables us to still function when the sun goes down.

A warm light in a window welcomes weary family members home. A nightlight comforts a frightened child. Family pets search out sunbeams streaming through windows to find just the right spot for an afternoon nap. For centuries, sailors searched for the light of certain stars to guide them safely to shore. Lighthouses kept ships from running aground. We use flashlights to search for lost things under beds and behind dusty armoires.

Light is the source of beauty in our lives. Each color is a different wavelength of light. When the white light from the sun is separated through droplets of water, a rainbow fills the sky. Light streaming through stained-glass windows brightens a room.

When the sun's rays enter the earth's atmosphere, oxygen and nitrogen scatter light waves. The shorter blue and violet wavelengths are the most affected. As they are broken apart and radiate through the atmosphere from horizon to horizon, they give us our blue sky.

Light is used for observing important events. Twinkling lights on a Christmas tree, festive fireworks on the Fourth of July, and melting candles on a birthday cake are delightful ingredients to many celebrations.

We love light. It floods every corner of our lives.

The opening chapter of Genesis begins with the Creator speaking light into existence. Throughout the Old Testament, light is contrasted with darkness, emphasizing the distinction between good and evil. Light is also used to indicate life triumphing over death. In Psalm 56, the psalmist asks to be delivered from falling so he can walk in the "light of life."

David used light as a way of illustrating God's favor and protection. "The LORD is my light and my salvation—whom shall I fear?" (Psalm 27:1).

The prophet Isaiah foretold a day when gloom and despair would be banished for God's people. "The people walking in darkness have seen a great light; on those living in the land of deep darkness a light has dawned" (Isaiah 9:2).

John 1:9 describes the fulfillment of Isaiah's prophecy at the birth of Jesus as the light that "was coming into the world."

When we think of the pervasiveness of light and how essential it is to our very existence, it is fitting that Jesus said, "I am the light of the world" (John 8:12).

He is. He dispels our darkness. He warms our hearts. The light of His truth transfers us from the kingdom of darkness into the light of His presence.

He comforts. He heals. He guides. He reveals. He gives life. He delights. He brings beauty. He illuminates. He welcomes.

I pray that my grandchildren will understand that Jesus is the light of the world. May their lives be impacted by His glorious light.

Let Us Pray That . . .

- our grandchildren will believe that God himself is the Father of Light and the giver of all good things (James 1:17; 1 John 1:5).

- our grandchildren understand that God's Word gives light (Psalm 119:130).

- our grandchildren will believe in the light and become children of the light (1 Thessalonians 5:5).

- our grandchildren let their light shine to the glory of God (Matthew 5:16).

- our grandchildren refrain from grumbling and disputing so that they will shine like the stars in the heavens as they hold to the word of life (Philippians 2:15).

- our grandchildren look forward to the city whose light comes from the glory of God (Revelation 21:23).

Gracious and Loving God of Light, Jesus is the light of the world. So often, I miss the meaning of these words. Make me aware of everything this name for Jesus can mean in my life and in the lives of my loved ones. I thank you for the Light of the World, who came to be born as a tiny baby. I am grateful that we, the people who lived in darkness, have seen the great light. I pray for those who love darkness rather than light. May they have a change of heart and experience the freedom that comes from embracing the light. I ask, Father, that my grandchildren would grasp the reality that Jesus is the light of the world. May they experience the healing, comfort, guidance, and illumination that He brings. Let your light permeate every area of their lives. May they live as children of light. Amen.

Think and Do

- Do you have a first- or second-grade grandchild who enjoys science? Read *On a Beam of Light: A Story of Albert Einstein*. Use it as a springboard for talking to your grandchild about the wonders of light and Einstein's childhood curiosity.

- *Jesus Is the Light of the World: The Life of Jesus* is a beautifully illustrated book by the Newbery Award winner Katherine Paterson.

- First Peter 2:9 describes believers as a "chosen people, a royal priesthood, a holy nation, God's special possession" called "out of darkness into his wonderful light." What did you leave behind when God called you out of darkness? What does it feel like to know you are living in God's marvelous light? How can you live more fully as a child of light?

- Listen and meditate on the words of Handel's *Messiah*, especially the aria, "The People That Walked in Darkness." Listen for the gloom, and then note how it is lifted with the words "upon them has the light shined."

"Every good and perfect gift is from above, coming down from the Father of the heavenly lights, who does not change like shifting shadows" (James 1:17).

"This is the message we have heard from him and declare to you: God is light; in him there is no darkness at all" (1 John 1:5).

"The unfolding of your words gives light; it gives under-standing to the simple" (Psalm 119:130).

"You are all children of the light and children of the day. We do not belong to the night or to the darkness" (1 Thes-salonians 5:5).

"In the same way, let your light shine before others, that they may see your good deeds and glorify your Father in heaven" (Matthew 5:16).

"That you may become blameless and pure, 'children of God without fault in a warped and crooked generation.' Then you will shine among them like stars in the sky" (Philippians 2:15).

"The city does not need the sun or the moon to shine on it, for the glory of God gives it light, and the Lamb is its lamp" (Revelation 21:23).

day forty-nine:
I CHOOSE GENTLENESS

I choose gentleness. Nothing is won by
force. I choose to be gentle.
If I raise my voice may it be only in praise.
If I clench my fist, may it be only in prayer.
If I make a demand, may it be only of myself.

Max Lucado

Let your gentleness be evident to all. The Lord is near.

Philippians 4:5

It was nearly perfect—four deep drawers, solidly built, with a spacious top for brushes, combs, and pretty bracelets. So what if peeling paint and missing knobs were part of the bargain? This garage sale discovery was perfect for the room our three little girls shared.

I assured my skeptical husband that with a little effort and a small investment we could restore it to just like new.

Armed with an antiquing kit from True Value, I attacked the dresser with determination. Stripping the old paint was harder than I thought. Preparing it for new paint was painfully time-consuming. Spending hours in the garage was not my idea of fun—especially when swings needed pushing and hair needed braiding and a blue-eyed boy longed to play catch.

My patience wore thin. Together my husband and I hurried the process. With relief, we moved the finished product, complete with a green antique finish and new wooden knobs, into the girls' room.

Serving as hitching posts for imaginary horses tethered with jump ropes, the knobs soon loosened and rolled under the bed to join barrettes, Barbie shoes, and dust bunnies. When the paint began to peel, dark brown patches came through the green finish; the camouflage effect made it look like it belonged with my son's GI Joe collection. I concluded that furniture restoration was not my thing. As Christian believers, our thing should be restoring people—significantly harder and slower than restoring furniture.

Addressing the legalistic, quick-fix Galatians, Paul gave a prescription for restoring individuals in Christ: "Brothers and sisters, if someone is caught in a sin, you who live by the Spirit should restore that person gently. But watch yourselves, or you also may be tempted. Carry each other's burdens, and in this way you will fulfill the law of Christ" (Galatians 6:1–2).

These words from Paul, and my brief encounter with sandpaper, have taught me many valuable lessons about restoration.

The word Paul uses for *restore* in this passage is the same word used in the Gospels for mending fishing nets. The meaning is clear. An individual should be restored to former usefulness. Restoration isn't about obtaining outward conformity but about assisting an individual until "Christ is formed" in him or her. The goal is to help each person (including our children and grandchildren) become the unique individual God created that person to be, fulfilling God's purpose for life, living in the freedom and fellowship and grace of Jesus Christ.

The issue is who God wants each person to be, not what we want.

Restoration cannot be rushed. This means we can't restore anyone by slapping on a figurative coat of paint to make him or her look presentable. That was the Galatians' problem. They confused outward conformity with inner transformation.

Patience and respect are crucial to genuine restoration. Understanding an individual's unique history is essential so that the restoration process will work "with the grain" of that person and what he or she may have experienced. Before it can begin, layers of old hurts, misconceptions, and lies may need to be stripped. Wounds and scratches must be discovered and healed. This takes time.

Most important, restoration requires gentleness. At times we come at people, especially family members, with an electric sander when the gentle hand rubbing of extra fine steel wool is required. We pound away with nails when a dab of strategically placed wood glue would do the job. Even worse, we come vigorously swinging a chain, as if we're trying to achieve the distressed and weathered look—great for some decors but much too brutal for flesh and blood and already dented souls.

Harsh words, abrupt confrontations, and heartless advice can cause greater damage, so that another person has to work harder to help genuine restoration take place. There is a cure for our lack of gentleness; it's the gentleness of Christ. In Matthew 11:29, He offers us the greatest bargain of all time: "Take my yoke upon you and learn from me, for I am gentle and humble in heart, and you will find rest for your souls."

When my mother moved from her large home into a small apartment, she needed to make the hard decisions about what to keep and what to discard. One of the few pieces of furniture that remained was my grandfather's desk. I remember my white-haired, very round grandfather hunched over that desk working on "the books" with a No. 2 pencil. The first book I read from cover to cover, *The Two Marys,* sat on the little bookshelf above the desk.

Pa's 75-year-old desk had some scratches, nicks, and wobbly legs. Hopefully, someday someone will want to restore it to its original beauty and usefulness. If they do, they will need to call in an expert who will work on this fragile piece of furniture with the gentleness and respect it deserves.

The children and grandchildren God brings into our lives are precious to Him. Should we ever need to help them be restored, we need to proceed with caution. Our job is not to fix or scold them. Our job is to encourage and restore them with the gentleness and humility of Christ.

My prayer is that I as a grandparent will always respond to my grandchildren's need for correction with gentleness and tenderness. I pray as well that they will learn to be gentle, kind, compassionate, and tender people.

Let Us Pray That . . .

- we and our grandchildren will learn to respond to anger with gentleness (Proverbs 15:1).
- our grandchildren receive others with the gentleness of Christ (Mark 10:13–16).
- our grandchildren exhibit gentleness as a fruit of the Spirit (Galatians 5:22–23).
- our grandchildren pursue gentleness (1 Timothy 6:11).
- our grandchildren will learn gentleness from Jesus (Matthew 11:29).

Master Restorer, thank you for the hundreds of times you have restored my soul. I thank you for your Holy Spirit, who works with us so gently to instruct, encourage, and nudge us into paths of righteousness. I thank you for your discipline, which often seems harsh but is meant to refine and restore. Help us to understand that your discipline is actually an act of kindness. Use us in our grandchildren's lives to bring gentle restoration. Help us to follow Paul's advice to watch ourselves so we can avoid the same temptations. Give us true humility as we love and correct family members. When we do not know how to help a struggling grandchild, remind us that you, the master restorer, can be our help and guide. May our grandchildren learn to be gentle in all of their relationships, for the Lord is near. Amen.

Think and Do

- Have you ever needed restoration? How were you approached? Did the approach of the "restorer" make a difference in how you responded?
- In 1 Thessalonians 2, Paul describes the ministry he had among the Thessalonians. He reminded them that he was as

gentle with them as a nursing mother caring for her child. Read the entire chapter and make a list of the characteristics of Paul's ministry. How can you imitate his gentleness in your home, work, neighborhood, and church?

• Who doesn't love Ferdinand the bull? Gentle Ferdinand would rather smell flowers than fight. *The Story of Ferdinand* by Munro Leaf is a children's classic.

"A gentle answer turns away wrath, but a harsh word stirs up anger" (Proverbs 15:1).

"And he took the children in his arms, placed his hands on them and blessed them" (Mark 10:16).

"But the fruit of the Spirit is love, joy, peace, forbearance, kindness, goodness, faithfulness, gentleness and self-control. Against such things there is no law" (Galatians 5:22–23).

"But you, man of God, flee from all this, and pursue righteousness, godliness, faith, love, endurance and gentleness" (1 Timothy 6:11).

"Take my yoke upon you and learn from me, for I am gentle and humble in heart, and you will find rest for your souls" (Matthew 11:29).

day fifty:
SMALL THINGS, GREAT LOVE

If you cannot do great things, do small things in a great way.

Napoleon Hill

Whoever can be trusted with very little can also be trusted with much.

Luke 16:10

According to public records that I've examined, Erving's Location, New Hampshire; Hibberts Gore, Maine; Holy City, California; Lost Springs, Wyoming; New Amsterdam, Indiana; and Monowi, Nebraska, share an attention-grabbing trait. At one time they were the six smallest towns in the USA—each reporting a population of one.

If your summer vacation includes a drive through one of these hamlets, you will want to slow down and heed the familiar warning, "Don't blink or you will miss it." These towns are tiny, but not trivial—at least not to the lonely resident. They are worthy of our attention.

As parents and grandparents, we take note of the small things. At first, it is fingers and toes, the shampooed fragrance of sleepy heads, the expression that reminds us of Grandpa, the smile that came from Dad, the first words that predict genius. Each small thing is worthy of our attention.

Yes, small things are important. The Bible tells us so.

Bethlehem was a small town. If you were in a hurry, as you clopped and bounced your way through the dusty streets on the back of a donkey, you just might miss it. Yet, as small as it was, Bethlehem was central in the fulfillment of prophecy. A great and beloved ruler came from this insignificant place. "But you, Bethlehem Ephrathah, though you are small among the clans of Judah, out of you will come for me one who will be ruler over Israel, whose origins are from of old, from ancient times" (Micah 5:2).

Jesus, when teaching about worldly possessions, asked His listeners to be faithful with whatever amount they had—no matter how small. "Whoever can be trusted with very little can also be trusted with much, and whoever is dishonest with very little will be dishonest with much" (Luke 16:10).

We all know what happened when a small boy shared his meager lunch with Jesus.

Even the small everyday habits of life are important and can bring glory to God. Paul put it like this: "So whether you eat or drink or whatever you do, do it all for the glory of God" (1 Corinthians 10:31).

We tend to overlook the importance of being faithful in the small things of life. We dream of doing great things for God. Words from Mother Teresa encourage us to see the value of small things: "Not all of us can do great things. But we can do small things with great love."

Jesus did small things with great love. He attended weddings. He welcomed children. He sat beside a well with an outcast and shared a cup of water. He washed his disciples' feet. He made breakfast on the shore. He embraced the small things of everyday life as a way of showing His love.

My prayer is that my grandchildren will see the value of small things. Through their lifetimes, may they have thousands of opportunities to faithfully do small things with great love.

Let Us Pray That . . .

- our grandchildren will live faithful lives and receive God's blessing (Proverbs 28:20).

- our grandchildren never forsake steadfast love and faithfulness (Proverbs 3:3).
- our grandchildren will do their work as if for the Lord rather than for people (Colossians 3:23).
- our granddaughters will see the tasks of homemaking as an opportunity to serve with love (Titus 2:4–5; Proverbs 31).
- our grandchildren will see the job of providing for a family as a way of showing love and being faithful to God.
- our grandchildren serve God faithfully and remember all that He has done for them (1 Samuel 12:24).
- our grandchildren will be diligent in using their spiritual gifts for the Lord (Romans 12:8).
- our grandchildren hear the words "well done" when they meet the Lord because they have been faithful in the small things (Matthew 25:23).

Father, thank you for the small, everyday gifts and opportunities you have entrusted to us. Help us grow in our faithfulness with the small things of life. May we be humble enough to do the little things that you were willing to do: serve, wash, welcome, touch, give, and love. We pray, Father, that in our materialistic and fame-obsessed world, our grandchildren will be able to sift through all the faulty messages and find great joy in simply serving others. May they see the tasks of everyday life as opportunities to be faithful and to express love. Be glorified in whatever they do. Amen.

Think and Do

- Read *Small Things with Great Love* by Margot Starbuck and consider how you can use small expressions of love to reach your friends and neighbors. Embark on an adventure with your grandchildren as together you find someone for whom you can do small things with great love.
- Are there any small things you have been avoiding? How can you express faithfulness to God by being faithful with the small stuff of life? Do you feel your gifts are too small

to make a difference? Remember the little boy with five loaves and two fish?

- Read 1 Thessalonians 4:11. How well does this admonition reflect our current Christian culture?

- Are there small things you can do to enrich your children's or grandchildren's lives? Perhaps you can be the "book" grandparent, giving them good literature as gifts. Or are you the "game" grandparent who spends hours playing board games? Find ways to do small things with great love.

"A faithful person will be richly blessed, but one eager to get rich will not go unpunished" (Proverbs 28:20).

"Let love and faithfulness never leave you; bind them around your neck, write them on the tablet of your heart" (Proverbs 3:3).

"Whatever you do, work at it with all your heart, as working for the Lord, not for human masters" (Colossians 3:23).

"Then they can urge the younger women to love their husbands and children, to be self-controlled and pure, to be busy at home, to be kind, and to be subject to their husbands, so that no one will malign the word of God" (Titus 2:4–5).

"But be sure to fear the LORD and serve him faithfully with all you heart; consider what great things he has done for you" (1 Samuel 12:24).

"If it is to encourage, then give encouragement; if it is giving, then give generously; if it is to lead, do it diligently; if it is to show mercy, do it cheerfully" (Romans 12:8).

"His master replied, 'Well done, good and faithful servant! You have been faithful with a few things; I will put you in charge of many things. Come and share your master's happiness!' " (Matthew 25:23).

day fifty-one:
ONE WILD AND PRECIOUS LIFE

You are not here in the world for yourself. You have been sent here for others. The world is waiting for you.

Catherine Booth

For we are God's handiwork, created in Christ Jesus to do good works, which God prepared in advance for us to do.

Ephesians 2:10

For years, Ma and Pa Ingalls showed up at our house on Sunday evenings. The girls always came with them. While our own kids ate pizza or munched on popcorn, we cheered on the family with each new trial they faced. When Nellie acted like a snobbish bully, we rooted for Laura and celebrated when the grocer's daughter received her just desserts. When Mary contracted scarlet fever and lost her sight, we all cried. Some of us sobbed. When Albert came to live with the family, we were inspired by Pa's ability to love the boy as if he were his own son.

I've read that Laura Ingalls Wilder didn't start writing until she was in her forties and didn't publish until her sixties. I am so grateful she persevered. Her *Little House* books have touched the hearts of millions of boys and girls, teaching them about love, family, morality, sacrifice, and faith. The world is a better place because of her work.

Anna Mary Robertson Moses claimed she began her painting career in her seventies to create a Christmas gift for her postman. She said painting was easier than baking a cake. For years, she had done embroidery and quilting, but arthritis had made holding a small needle painful. Choosing painting as a medium for her creativity was natural. Over the next three decades, Grandma Moses created more than 1,600 paintings. Her folk art can be found in museums throughout America.

Some develop their gifts and strengths earlier in life. Olympic athletes begin as young as age three to maximize their athletic gifts. Serious musicians almost always began their study of music in the preschool years. Children with a bent toward engineering or the sciences find ways to nurture this as they excel in math studies or design buildings from Legos. More and more young people are taking an active interest in the culinary arts. A strength for understanding and loving other cultures is propelling thousands of young people into serving outside of the United States as English as a Second Language teachers.

Not every gift and strength is related to the arts or to a profession. Not every talent is visible. Some people possess internal and relational strengths that allow them to quietly and powerfully serve others.

Each of my grandchildren has different internal strengths. Samantha is sweet and imaginative. Madelyn is quiet and determined. Holden is curious and cuddly. Kevin is a thinker. He remembers everything he reads. Nicole is relational and kind.

The gifts of thinking, problem solving, and compassion have served one friend well as she and her husband have been the primary advocates for their autistic son. Her perseverance has enabled him to walk a safe and productive life path.

Cheryl's love and expertise in the field of children's literature has assisted many people as they look for resources to use in the classroom or in the family. The information my friend shares is priceless. Our bookshelves are filled with her recommendations.

Our daughter-in-law's father, Lee, has blended his history as the son of a farmer in South Dakota with his own talent for gardening to create Plymouth Rock Farm. In the spring, summer, and fall, he spends his evenings and weekends caring for his own massive garden. The produce that doesn't go to the farmers' market is shared with friends and family in the form of pizza sauce, plum jam, applesauce, and a variety of other canned goods he cooks up with his wife, Janet. Our pantry has been blessed by the abundance of Lee and Janet's garden. One year, Lee surprised us with a trunk full of pumpkins to share with our grandkids.

One woman's love for homemaking and gift of organization has resulted in a home that is welcoming and inviting to her husband, their girls, and their many friends. Her strengths have allowed her children to flourish in a stable and loving environment. She is a model for young moms who share the same dream for a healthy, happy family.

Without exception, every person has been made in the image of God. Each life is precious and filled with promise. It is our job, with the Lord's help, to discover and develop our potential.

Author Mary Oliver asks this searching question, "Tell me, what is it that you plan to do with your one wild and precious life?" Life is an extravagant gift. Let's not waste it.

I have three prayers for my grandchildren on this topic.

I pray that they will embrace the wonderful gift of life and make every effort to explore their gifts and abilities and develop those gifts throughout their lives.

I pray that they will realize that these gifts are not simply for their own self-fulfillment but are to be used to benefit others.

The Right to Life organization reports there were 1.1 million abortions in America in 2013. More than one million babies were robbed of their wild and precious life. Our nation has been robbed of their presence and gifts.

According to Robert P. George, author of *Embryo: A Defense of Human Life*, at the moment of conception the embryo becomes a "whole, self-directed organism." In other words, it contains within itself all the information that is needed to mature into a fully formed human being filled with potential.

My final prayer is that my grandchildren will use their own potential to support the cause of the unborn, who have a right to live out their own precious lives.

Let Us Pray That . . .

- our grandchildren see life as a gift to be cherished (Genesis 2:7).

- our grandchildren understand that God formed and knows them (Psalm 139:13–18).

- our grandchildren understand that God has work for them to do (Ephesians 2:10).

- our grandchildren will recognize their spiritual gifts (Romans 12:6–8; 1 Corinthians 12).

- our grandchildren will use their gifts with humility (Philippians 2:3).

- our grandchildren understand the Christian's responsibility to help the helpless (Proverbs 24:11–12).

Giver of Life, you have given all of us the most precious of gifts — life. Help us to value our time here on earth and to live out this adventure with joy. I pray that you will help us as we encourage our grandchildren to explore their interests and develop their strengths. We know that you have created each with unique temperaments, gifts, and talents. May they use these gifts to serve others and glorify you. We pray, Lord, for the end to abortion. We mourn the loss of so many children. We confess this sin to you and ask for your forgiveness. May our grandchildren's generation fight for the right to life. Amen.

Think and Do

- Read Psalm 92:12–15. How do these verses encourage you today? How can you continue to bear fruit even when you enter retirement? Are there gifts and talents that have been neglected? Is there something you have always wanted to try?

- Make a list of the gifts, talents, and strengths you see in each child. Remember that not all strengths are highly visible. Some are internal. Set aside a time with each grandchild so you can look for clues to internal strengths such as compassion, mercy, kindness, thoughtfulness, love of reading, sense of humor, creativity, bravery, determination, justice, and imagination to name a few. Be sure to affirm the strengths you see.

- *Oh, the Places You'll Go!* by Dr. Seuss is a favorite in many families. It is a great gift for a child entering kindergarten or graduating from high school.

"Then the LORD God formed a man from the dust of the ground and breathed into his nostrils the breath of life, and the man became a living being" (Genesis 2:7).

"Your eyes saw my unformed body; all the days ordained for me were written in your book before one of them came to be" (Psalm 139:16).

"For we are God's handiwork, created in Christ Jesus to do good works, which God prepared in advance for us to do" (Ephesians 2:10).

"We have different gifts, according to the grace given to each of us. If your gift is prophesying, then prophesy in accordance with your faith; if it is serving, then serve; if it is teaching, then teach; if it is to encourage, then give encouragement; if it is giving, then give generously; if it is to lead, do it diligently; if it is to show mercy, do it cheerfully (Romans 12:6–8).

"Do nothing out of selfish ambition or vain conceit. Rather, in humility value others above yourselves" (Philippians 2:3).

"Rescue those being led away to death" (Proverbs 24:11).

day fifty-two:
SPENDING HABITS

What does love look like? It has the hands to help others. It
has the feet to hasten to the poor and needy. It has eyes to see
misery and want. It has the ears to hear the sighs and sorrows
of men. That is what love looks like.

Augustine

And if you spend yourselves in behalf of the hungry and satisfy
the needs of the oppressed, then your light will rise in the darkness, and your night will become like the noonday.

Isaiah 58:10

Socks. I waste money on socks.

We had four children in six years. On laundry day, it could
take an hour to sort the little socks heaped in the laundry basket.
More than once, I became so overwhelmed with the chore of
sorting socks and looking for lost mates that I dumped all the
socks into a garbage bag and stashed it in a closet. Starting
over with new socks from our local department store seemed
like the only option.

A waste of money? Yes. Sort of silly? Absolutely. Did it save
my sanity? You bet.

Honestly, the sock incident was not nearly as serious as some
of my other spending disasters. Spending our resources wisely
is not a strength for me. That is a nice way of saying I still make
a mess of it from time to time.

I suspect my greatest spending mistake is not what I spend money on but rather what I *don't* spend my money on. Isaiah 58:10 is convicting: "If you spend yourselves in behalf of the hungry and satisfy the needs of the oppressed, then your light will rise in the darkness, and your night will become like the noonday."

Spending ourselves on behalf of the poor is hard to understand. What does that look like?

Vaclav was the Duke of Bohemia in the 900s. Until his assassination by his brother, Vaclav dedicated his life to the Christianization of what is now the Czech Republic.

A legend tells us that on Christmas Day he would tuck a gold coin into the hand of each of his servants and give them a blessing. "May the Lord Jesus Christ, our Saviour who was born on this day, bless you and watch over you."[16]

The tale goes on to say that a peasant observed this Christmas Day ritual. He challenged the Duke on his seeming hypocrisy: Giving gold coins to your servants who are well fed and warm is one thing. What have you done about the poor who have no clothing, no food, and are living in shacks on Christmas Day?

Moved by the condition of the local peasants, Vaclav called his servant to venture out with him into the cold that Christmas Day. The Duke wanted to visit those in greatest need. Vaclav and the servant didn't dress warmly enough for the cold, but carrying food for the poor, they trudged on and made it all the way to St. Agnes Fountain. There they found an old woman breaking ice in the fountain, hoping to get water. His heart was broken for the desperate condition of the people in that town.

Vaclav became recognized in the neighboring villages for his compassionate work. We have come to know him as Good King Wenceslas.

Homelessness is epidemic in some areas of our country. Driving the streets of many towns, we see men and women without warm coats in spite of extreme cold. One woman carries old coats in the back of her car to offer to the homeless she sees. Another person keeps a supply of fast-food gift certificates to hand out rather than giving money. One young lady goes to shop at a local dollar store and puts matching gloves and hats into plastic bags to give away to people in need. Food pantries are always in need of financial support and actual food contributions. My sister regularly works at a soup kitchen and has come to love the people who visit there. As poverty increases in our country, the need for volunteers for staffing these ministries increases as well.

Even with participating in a variety of creative ways, we are only scratching the surface of the needs that exist in our world.

C. S. Lewis' words on charitable giving from *Mere Christianity* challenge me: "I am afraid the only safe rule is to give more than we can spare. . . . If our charities do not at all pinch or hamper us . . . they are too small. There ought to be things we should like to do and cannot because our charitable expenditures excludes them."[17]

That sounds like spending oneself on behalf of the poor.

Maybe Lewis' philosophy of charitable giving is extreme. Maybe not. But I do know that God wants us to carefully consider our giving and to give cheerfully (2 Corinthians 9:7).

I pray that my grandchildren's eyes will be open to the needs around them. I pray they will have unselfish hearts and open hands and that their spending habits will reflect wisdom and compassion for the poor.

> Therefore, Christian men be sure,
> Wealth or rank possessing,
> Ye who now will bless the poor
> Shall yourself find blessing.
> —John Mason Neale

Let Us Pray That . . .

- our grandchildren will be generous to the needy and experience God's blessing (Proverbs 19:17).

- our grandchildren will learn to share what they have with others (Hebrews 13:16).

- our grandchildren will not close their hearts to those in need (1 John 3:17).

- our grandchildren give generously (2 Corinthians 9:7).

235

- our grandchildren understand that when they give to those who are considered the least in this world, they are giving to Jesus (Matthew 25:40).

Lord, thank you for the ways you meet our needs so abundantly. We recognize that we are among the richest people in the world. Help us to use the resources you have entrusted to us to not only meet the needs of our own families but also to bring hope and encouragement to others in need. Reorder our priorities and help us to teach our grandchildren the importance of spending themselves on behalf of the poor and hurting. May they grasp the concept that it is better to lay up treasures in heaven than to increase our wealth on earth. We pray for your mercy and grace for those who are struggling financially today. May they turn to you for their needs. May we be the answer to their prayers. Amen.

Think and Do

- *An Orange for Frankie* by Patricia Polacco is a great book to share with your grandchildren at Christmas. The main character experiences the joy of sharing what he has with a homeless man and learns an important lesson.
- Collect nonperishable items for a local food pantry. Take your grandkids along as you drop off your donations. Find a nearby soup kitchen and donate a few days a year to helping. Visit a food packing station for an organization such as Feed My Starving Children.

"Whoever is kind to the poor lends to the LORD, and he will reward them for what they have done" (Proverbs 19:17).

"And do not forget to do good and to share with others, for with such sacrifices God is pleased" (Hebrews 13:16).

"If anyone has material possessions and sees a brother or sister in need but has no pity on them, how can the love of God be in that person?" (1 John 3:17).

"Each of you should give what you have decided in your heart to give, not reluctantly or under compulsion, for God loves a cheerful giver" (2 Corinthians 9:7).

"The King will reply, 'Truly I tell you, whatever you did for one of the least of these brothers and sisters of mine, you did for me' " (Matthew 25:40).

day fifty-three:
DEEP AND WIDE

I actually think that God wants the church to be reformed by the reading of the Scripture.

N. T. Wright

Do not conform to the pattern of this world, but be transformed by the renewing of your mind.

Romans 12:2

I heard of a pastor with an unusually effective ministry. In fact, it was so effective that fellow pastors relentlessly interrogated him for some clue to the secret of his success. Repeatedly, the pastor shook his head and told his friends he had no secret program or system to explain the spiritual growth and maturity he was witnessing in his congregation. He could offer them no formula for obtaining the same success.

One day, when grilled again, he humbly replied, "The only thing I can think of is that I read through the entire New Testament every week."

Have you heard Joseph Stowell say that we should read the Bible deep and wide? Deep for study. Wide to get a sense of God's redemptive plan for man.

I love both.

A Bible, a stack of commentaries, a concordance, a quiet house, and a cup of tea is my idea of a just-right morning. Searching deep into Scripture for treasure feeds my soul.

I have discovered that setting aside time to read large portions of Scripture is equally important to my spiritual growth.

On the few occasions when I attempt to read through the New Testament or Gospels in a short period of time, I always walk away with a deeper love for God's Word.

Reading large portions reaffirms my belief that God's Word is truth. Christians who commit to reading the Bible through each year often close their Bibles on December 31 having reached this conclusion: "It is true. It is all true." The continuity of the message is astounding, and it strengthens our faith.

In Psalm 19:7, the psalmist declared, "The law of the LORD is perfect, refreshing the soul." Reading through the New Testament, especially the Gospels, I am astonished by the perfection of the teaching of Jesus. Not even secularists can quibble with one word of the Sermon on the Mount. The most callous of hearts cannot dispute His words to the woman caught in adultery. Everyone cheers at his rebuke to the merchants in the temple. Even people of other faiths are stunned and moved by the Savior's statement of forgiveness at the cross.

They may reject His deity, but they cannot escape the truth of His teachings.

When I read through the Gospels in a short period of time, I imagine I have some of the same feelings as the disciples after Jesus had taught at a synagogue in Capernaum. That day, many turned away from the most difficult teachings of Jesus. They would follow Him no more. Turning to His closest followers, the Master asked if they were going to go as well. Simon Peter replied, "Lord, to whom shall we go? You have the words of eternal life" (John 6:68).

Whether we read deep or wide, God's Word can transform us, instruct us, comfort us, encourage us, and challenge us. These are the words of eternal life.

We must pray that the next generation of Christians will love God's Word and read it deep and wide. May they share the words of eternal life with a world in need.

Let Us Pray That . . .

- our grandchildren will know that all Scripture comes from God (2 Timothy 3:16).

239

- our grandchildren understand that throughout history not one good promise of God has failed (1 Kings 8:56).
- our grandchildren allow Christ's message to dwell in them richly and will share it with others (Colossians 3:16).
- our grandchildren will be built up by God's Word (Acts 20:32).
- our grandchildren love God's law and meditate on it (Psalm 119).
- our grandchildren will be doers of the Word (James 1:22).
- our grandchildren's lives will be transformed as their minds are renewed by God's Word (Romans 12:2).

Lord, your Word is a lamp to our feet and a light to our path. This light shines more brightly with each passing year. Your law is perfect. Your Word is sweet. Forgive us for so often neglecting your Word. We pray that our grandchildren will grow in their love for the Bible. May their generation embrace your Word for instruction in faith and life. We ask, Father, that they would learn to read your Word deep and wide. Through reading, may they gain an understanding of who you are and grasp your great love for them. As you speak to them through your Word, may they become doers and not hearers only. May your Word light their paths. Amen.

Think and Do

- In Corrie ten Boom's first book *The Hiding Place,* she remembers dinner times at her family home. Papa ten Boom always read Scripture before the meal. When she was later imprisoned, the Word of God, spoken at that dinner table so many years before, came back to strengthen her and give her hope. One verse in particular became her theme: "You are my hiding place" (Psalm 32:7). What verse of Scripture do you hope your grandchildren will remember in times of trouble? Can you read it before meals when they spend time with you?

- *The Bible Smuggler* by Louise A. Vernon is the story of William Tyndale. Published in 1967, it is a book that has been read by thousands of children. A good read-aloud selection, it will help your grandchildren understand the sacrifices made to bring God's Word to us.

- Consider planning a Bible reading retreat. Set aside time to read through the Gospels in a couple of days. Journal what you discover as you immerse yourself in the teachings of Jesus.

- My first complete Bible was a white, leather-bound, red-letter edition given to me by my grandmother at graduation. The pages are turning brown and falling away from the binding, but I still have that precious Bible. Do your grandchildren have their own Bible? Would that be a good gift for an up-coming special occasion?

"All Scripture is God-breathed and is useful for teaching, rebuking, correcting and training in righteousness" (2 Timothy 3:16).

"Praise be to the LORD, who has given rest to his people Israel just as he promised. Not one word has failed of all the good promises he gave through his servant Moses" (1 Kings 8:56).

"Let the message of Christ dwell among you richly as you teach and admonish one another with all wisdom through psalms, hymns, and songs from the Spirit, singing to God with gratitude in your hearts" (Colossians 3:16)

"Now I commit you to God and to the word of his grace, which can build you up and give you an inheritance among all those who are sanctified" (Acts 20:32).

"I meditate on your precepts and consider your ways. I delight in your decrees; I will not neglect your word" (Psalm 119:15–16).

"Do not merely listen to the word, and so deceive yourselves. Do what it says" (James 1:22).

"Do not conform to the pattern of this world, but be transformed by the renewing of your mind. Then you will be able to test and approve what God's will is—his good, pleasing and perfect will" (Romans 12:2).

day fifty-four:
TEMPO GIUSTO

This time, like all times, is a very good one. If we but know what to do with it.

Ralph Waldo Emerson

Since ancient times no one has heard,
no ear has perceived,
no eye has seen any God besides you,
who acts on behalf of those who wait for him.

Isaiah 64:4

Adagio in Strings by Samuel Barber is one of the most recognized orchestral pieces of the twentieth century. If you listened to it today, you would probably exclaim, "I've heard this before!" The haunting melody and slow tempo convey love, sorrow, suffering, and tenderness. Barber wrote an unforgettable composition.

Great composers select tempos with care. Samuel Barber's choice of *adagio* for this piece was no accident. The tempo set the mood. From the moment he wrote the first notes for the lower violins, he must have known this piece would be *Adagio in Strings*.

The often-used tempos: *adagio*, *lento*, and *allegro* determine not only the pace but also the emotional tone of musical compositions.

There is a lesser-known tempo used as a notation by Italian composers—*tempo giusto*. In Gail Godwin's book *Heart*, she offers a personal interpretation of "tempo giusto" and encourages her readers to incorporate the theory into everyday life.

"The Italians have a musical notation not found in any other language: tempo giusto, 'the right tempo.' It means a steady, normal beat, between 66 and 76 on the metronome. Tempo giusto is the appropriate beat of the human heart."[18]

Just the right tempo. What a concept! Imagine the serenity we would experience if we could find the right speed at which to live the masterpiece of our lives. The very thought brings peace and calm.

I rarely live at *tempo giusto*. In fact, I have created my own terminology for the pace at which I live.

Tempo *frantico*!

Yes, I hurry here and rush there. I rarely stop to take time to listen to God—much less wait on Him. I neglect relationships. I compromise my physical and emotional health. Just thinking of it raises my pulse and blood pressure.

There is a "right tempo" for life, a steady, unhurried beat that allows the masterpiece to come to life. Our choice of tempo sets the pace at which we live. Our choice sets the emotional tone for our relationships.

My grandparents understood *tempo giusto*. Hot summer days slid by while they sipped sweating glasses of iced tea. Spending hours parked in metal lawn chairs, they swatted mosquitoes and watched little girls in sundresses chase fireflies.

There was always time for a game of cards or one more story. Hanging sheets on the line was not a task to be done but an opportunity to smell fresh laundry and laugh at the billowing fabric. Flowers were meant to be sniffed, admired, and arranged in vases. Puddles were for splashing. Umbrellas waited by the door, eager for three little girls to take a walk in the rain while Grandma recited, "Rain, rain go away." A piece of chocolate cake was an event to be shared. Doing the dishes meant singing in harmony and lingering over a sink filled with bubbles. Naps were a must.

It was in this world of observing *tempo giusto* that I learned how to wait on and listen for God.

The fourth commandment tells us to "Remember the Sabbath day by keeping it holy" (Exodus 20:8).

A day of rest. What at a concept! Just the thought of it brings peace and calm. The Master Composer has inserted a notation of *tempo giusto* into our *allegro* lives.

My husband has called the Sabbath a day of "paid vacation." He is correct. It is a gift. It is meant to benefit and strengthen us. When Jesus was criticized by the Pharisees for allowing His disciples to pick some grain on the Sabbath, He told them, "The Sabbath was made for man, not man for the Sabbath" (Mark 2:27).

Whatever day we observe the Sabbath, we are living at *tempo giusto*. On that day, we are living life at the right speed for re-connecting with God and our loved ones.

One of the blessings of being grandparents is that, for many of us, our daily responsibilities have lightened. When we enter retirement, we have more freedom to live life at just the right speed for welcoming grandchildren. We can be an example to our grandchildren of the benefits of living at *tempo giusto* rather than *frantico*. We can model what Mark Buchanan in his book *The Rest of God* calls a Sabbath heart. "A Sabbath heart," he wrote, "is restful even in the midst of unrest and upheaval."

My prayer is that my grandchildren will embrace the concept of the Sabbath. I pray that they will manage their days in a way that will allow them the time to enjoy the world God has given to them. May they live at just the right speed and learn to wait on God.

Let Us Pray That . . .

- our grandchildren will realize that God wants to give His people rest (Exodus 33:14).

- our grandchildren understand that Jesus invites them to come to Him for rest (Matthew 11:28).

- our grandchildren will know that true rest can be found in God alone (Psalm 62:1–2).

- our grandchildren understand that the Sabbath is a gift to them (Mark 2:27).

- our grandchildren take the time to wait upon the LORD (Psalm 130:5–6; Isaiah 40:31).
- our grandchildren seek the Lord and His beauty as they live at the right speed (Psalm 27:4–5).
- our grandchildren's hearts will be at Sabbath rest even in turbulent times (Psalm 27:1; Isaiah 41:10).

Lord of the Sabbath, forgive us for not accepting the gift of rest you have provided. Forgive us for dashing around as if we are in charge of the universe. Help us to trust you completely so we will take time to slow down and rest. Father, our grandchildren are growing up in a world rushing by them at a frantic pace. They are being told that their worth and value is linked to how much they get done and achieve. Make our homes a sanctuary where these children can experience life at just the right speed. Teach them the value of quiet times so they can grow closer to you. Lord, we pray for a Sabbath heart, a heart that is at rest no matter what is going on around us. Amen.

Think and Do

- My husband and I have learned much from *The Rest of God*, Mark Buchanan's book on the Sabbath. You may discover a fresh way of looking at the Sabbath through Mr. Buchanan's writing.
- How are you doing with the idea of living at the right speed? Is there a way to simplify your life so you can live with greater peace? Are there leisurely activities you can do with your grandchildren that will allow their hearts and souls to rest?
- *A Quiet Place* by Douglas Wood might open up conversation with your grandchild about where they go to slow down and be quiet.

"The LORD replied, 'My Presence will go with you, and I will give you rest' " (Exodus 33:14).

"Come to me, all you who are weary and burdened, and I will give you rest" (Matthew 11:28).

"Truly my soul finds rest in God; my salvation comes from him. Truly he is my rock and my salvation; he is my fortress, I will never be shaken" (Psalm 62:1–2).

"Then he said to them, 'The Sabbath was made for man, not man for the Sabbath' " (Mark 2:27).

"I wait for the LORD, my whole being waits, and in his word I put my hope" (Psalm 130:5).

"Those who hope in the LORD will renew their strength. They will soar on wings like eagles; they will run and not grow weary, they will walk and not be faint" (Isaiah 40:31).

"One thing I ask from the LORD, this only do I seek: that I may dwell in the house of the LORD all the days of my life, to gaze on the beauty of the LORD and to seek him in his temple" (Psalm 27:4).

"The LORD is my light and my salvation—whom shall I fear? The LORD is the stronghold of my life—of whom shall I be afraid?" (Psalm 27:1).

day fifty-five:
TREES AND TRAINS

A tree grows because it adds rings: a train doesn't grow by leaving one station behind and puffing on to the next.

C. S. Lewis

Grow in the grace and knowledge of our Lord and Savior Jesus Christ.

2 Peter 3:18

My mother was just a little girl when my grandparents planted the tree. By the time we played in its shade, it was engulfing the small front yard. In the fall, the leaves filled the gutters and littered the sidewalk. The decaying leaves created dust and dirt. We tracked all manner of debris into Grandmother's house. The roots twisted and burrowed underground causing the concrete driveway my grandfather had poured to crack and buckle.

The tree had to go. My sisters and I watched from Grandma's sunroom as men arrived to cut it down and amputate its limbs. They carried off the beautiful tree in bits and pieces thrown into the back of a truck.

The tree was gone, but for a time the stump remained. We went to pay our respects to the tree. I knelt beside my sister Susan as she pointed to the rings on the stump. She was older and wiser than I. After all, she had finished first grade.

I didn't miss a word as my curly haired sister told me we could tell the age of the tree by the number of rings. She started at the center and counted out. Then she reversed the process starting from the last ring and counting to the innermost ring. As I recall, with each count we came up with a different number. It didn't matter. I was enthralled with the mystery of how trees grow.

Some years, the rings are thin—indicating drought, extreme heat, or some other event that robbed the tree of nutrients. Other years, the rings are thicker and darker because of abundant rain and nutrients. The rings of a tree can tell us a great deal about the growing environment.

Writing about growth and change, C. S. Lewis contrasted trees and trains. Human nature would prefer that growth and change be like taking a trip on a train. You step on board at Union Station in Chicago and hop off at Grand Central in Times Square. You leave your problems and struggles behind like baggage and arrive at your destination before you know it. It is all very neat and tidy and pleasant.

Change and growth don't happen that way. Human beings grow from the inside out. This year's growth is laid down on top of last year's growth. We grow 365 days a year. Sometimes our growth is slight because of circumstances or lack of spiritual nutrition. Other times, our growth is robust and noticeable to others because our environment is ideal for that season of our lives.

Mostly, growth is slow. Change doesn't come easily. We may become discouraged, but there is comfort in knowing that growth is a process that requires patience.

We all know the frustration and pain that come from wanting our own growth and maturity to happen more quickly. We also grow impatient with others as change and growth come slowly in their lives. We agonize and worry that change may never come. We would prefer to buy others a ticket, hand their baggage to a conductor, put them on a train, and wave goodbye from a platform—all the while hoping they reach their destination on our timetable.

As we pray for our grandchildren, we must remember that they will not instantly develop the character qualities we so deeply desire. When we pray, we aren't putting them on a train so they can reach a specific destination. Day after day, they are growing in ways that are imperceptible to us. Day after day, we are growing in ways that are imperceptible to them.

When we pray, we are praying that their environment and relationship with God will be such that they can grow year after year after year and become people who are whole and holy.

Our job is not to worry. Our job is not to criticize. Our job is to be patient, supportive, and faithful in prayer.

Let Us Pray That . . .

- our grandchildren will grow in the grace and knowledge of Jesus Christ (2 Peter 3:18).
- we will understand that it is God who causes spiritual growth (1 Corinthians 3:7).
- our grandchildren mature in Jesus Christ by growing in knowledge (Ephesians 4:13).
- our grandchildren flourish like a tree planted by rivers of water (Psalm 1).
- our grandchildren invite God to examine their lives to see where growth is needed (Psalm 139:23).
- we will not be judgmental or critical when growth is slow and will accept people where they are (Romans 14:13).
- we will not be filled with anxiety but will trust that the Lord will complete his good work in our grandchildren's lives (Philippians 1:6).
- we will warn, exhort, encourage, help, and be patient with all people (1 Thessalonians 5:14).

Heavenly Father, you are the gardener who oversees our growth. Help us to be patient as we grow. Forgive us for becoming irritated with the cultivating, weeding, and pruning process that is necessary. We pray that our grandchildren will remain connected to you so they can have all they need to grow and to bear fruit for you. May we build them up when they are discouraged. Help us to be patient with them rather than judgmental. May we trust you and your work in their lives instead of being filled with anxiety. Teach us how we can contribute to a healthy environment in which they can grow into the people you want them to be. Amen.

Think and Do

- Henry Cloud says, "All growth is spiritual growth." His book *How People Grow* is a great resource for those of us who want to understand how true growth occurs.

- *Outside Your Window* by Nicola Davis opens up the world of nature to your grandchildren.

- Plant a tree with your grandchild. This project can be a learning experience for your grandchild and can be a reminder to you that growth comes slowly. Visit a local nursery or visit the National Arbor Day Foundation online.

"But grow in the grace and knowledge of our Lord and Savior Jesus Christ. To him be glory both now and forever! Amen" (2 Peter 3:18).

"That person is like a tree planted by streams of water, which yields its fruit in season and whose leaf does not wither—whatever they do prospers" (Psalm 1:3).

"Search me, God, and know my heart; test me and know my anxious thoughts" (Psalm 139:23).

"Therefore let us stop passing judgment on one another. Instead, make up your mind not to put any stumbling block or obstacle in the way of a brother or sister" (Romans 14:13).

"And we urge you, brothers and sisters, warn those who are idle and disruptive, encourage the disheartened, help the weak, be patient with everyone" (1 Thessalonians 5:14).

"Being confident of this, that he who began a good work in you will carry it on to completion until the day of Christ Jesus" (Philippians 1:6).

"Until we all reach unity in the faith and in the knowledge of the Son of God and become mature, attaining to the whole measure of the fullness of Christ" (Ephesians 4:13).

day fifty-six:
PRAYER PARTNERS

The single greatest reason why we are losing a generation is because the home is no longer the place of the transference of the faith. We live in a day of "outsourcing". . . Today, we have a generation of people that outsource their kids.

Tony Evans

I am reminded of your sincere faith, which first lived in your grandmother Lois and in your mother Eunice and, I am persuaded, now lives in you also.

2 Timothy 1:5

Miriam Welty was my first prayer partner. She was the wife of a former pastor who was the registrar at the college I attended, and she worked on campus as an administrative assistant. My freshman year, I manned the switchboard and spent a few hours each week in the Dean of Students office typing or filing.

During breaks, I would sit in a chair by Miriam's desk. She would turn off her IBM Selectric typewriter and spend time sharing recipes, asking me about classes, or telling me stories of her two sons. Her love for God and words of wisdom helped me adjust to new situations all during my college years.

On Fridays, I cleaned house for the Weltys. Miriam had the gift of hospitality. Every Sunday, Miriam and Herald invited college kids to their house for a home-cooked meal and to play board games. Part of my Friday duties was to bake cookies or cakes to be served at Sunday dinner. Miriam had a delicious recipe for applesauce chocolate chip cookies that I have lost over the years.

One Friday, as I dusted the coffee table, I picked up Miriam's tattered, green Living Bible. Her prayer list was poking out between the pages. I couldn't help but notice my name toward the top. Under my name she had listed many of the things about which I had expressed concern as I sat by her desk during breaks. Sometimes Miriam and I would pray together for my concerns. But now I knew she continued to pray for them in her daily quiet time.

Knowing that Miriam prayed for me solidified our friendship.

When Ray and I were married, Rev. Welty performed the ceremony. Mrs. Welty walked down the aisle as the mother of the bride. There are no words to describe how dearly we loved the Weltys.

In the book *Grandma, I Need Your Prayers,* authors Quin Sherrer and Ruthanne Garlock address the spiritual influence of grandparents. As they asked people to share the ways in which their grandmothers had influenced their lives, they found a consistent response: My grandma prayed.

One woman's memories of her grandmother especially stirred my heart. "She was my first prayer partner, and remembering the intimacy she had with the Lord has given me the security to know he is there for me when I call."

Intercessory prayer is a privilege. Bringing a Christian brother or sister's needs before the Lord is an honor. James 5:16 encourages us to pray for one another because "the prayer of a righteous person is powerful and effective."

As great a privilege as it is to pray for other believers, it is an even greater honor to pray for our grandchildren. Imagine the joy of being your grandchild's first prayer partner.

Could this be our highest calling?

After all these years of serving the Lord in various ministries, could our greatest work be the work of prayer? Is it possible that the work we do at this stage of life is as important as all that has gone before?

Psalm 92:14–15 says, "They will still bear fruit in old age, they will stay fresh and green, proclaiming, 'The LORD is upright.' "

May the Lord use us in the lives of our grandchildren. May we become so consistent in praying for them that they know they can rely on and trust us. Let us proclaim to our grandchildren through our commitment to prayer, "The LORD is upright."

Let Us Pray That . . .

- we learn to be interested in our grandchildren's concerns and take them seriously (Philippians 2:3–4).

- we remember that Jesus now lives to make intercession for us and our children and grandchildren (Hebrews 7:25).

- we remember to pray for our grandchildren rather than being anxious (Philippians 4:6–7; 1 Peter 5:7).

- we continue to pray for our grandchildren's concerns without ceasing and give thanks for what God is doing in their lives (1 Thessalonians 5:16–18).

- we will always pray and never give up (Luke 18:1).

- we recognize the reality that the Holy Spirit intercedes when we don't know how to pray for our grandchildren (Romans 8:26).

Heavenly Father, we thank you for the loving Christians who have prayed for us throughout our lives. Their prayers were a gift to us. Father, teach us how to pray so we can be effective and powerful as we bring our grandchildren's requests to you. Give us sensitivity to their concerns. Teach us to honor their privacy by not sharing their concerns with others. Help us to be consistent in our prayer lives, not only for our own growth but also so our grandchildren can truly trust us with their requests. Thank you for the opportunity and privilege of praying for these children. Lord, we want to be their prayer partners. Thank you that we can still be of use to you at this stage of life. May our prayer life keep us young and vibrant in spirit and bearing much fruit for your kingdom. Amen.

Think and Do

- *Grandma, I Need Your Prayers* by Quin Sherrer and Ruthanne Garlock contains many wonderful ideas about praying for your grandchildren.

- Prayer Bowls can be purchased online. These beautiful bowls can be left on the dining room table next to note cards and pens. Perhaps your grandchildren will quietly drop their requests in the bowl so you can pray for them during your own prayer time.

- In Mark Batterson's book *Praying Circles Around Your Children*, he talks about the difference between ASAP prayers and ALAIT prayers—"As Long As It Takes" prayers. Is there a family concern you have been praying about for years? What can you learn from Luke 18:1?

- Do you have a preschool grandchild who will listen for hours while you read? *One Year Devotions for Preschoolers* by Crystal Bowman might be a wonderful gift that will increase your spiritual influence.

"Do nothing out of selfish ambition or vain conceit. Rather, in humility value others above yourselves" (Philippians 2:3).

"Therefore he is able to save completely those who come to God through him, because he always lives to intercede for them" (Hebrews 7:25).

"Do not be anxious about anything, but in every situation, by prayer and petition, with thanksgiving, present your requests to God. And the peace of God, which transcends all understanding, will guard your hearts and your minds in Christ Jesus" (Philippians 4:6–7).

"Rejoice always, pray continually, give thanks in all circumstances; for this is God's will for you in Christ Jesus" (1 Thessalonians 5:16–18).

"Then Jesus told his disciples a parable to show them that they should always pray and not give up" (Luke 18:1).

"In the same way, the Spirit helps us in our weakness. We do not know what we ought to pray for, but the Spirit himself intercedes for us through wordless groans" (Romans 8:26).

day fifty-seven:
TRUST AND VERIFY

A lie can travel halfway round the world while truth is still lacing up her boots.

Unknown

Then you will know the truth, and the truth will set you free.

John 8:32

Orphaned at birth, Robert never knew his parents. He grew up in foster homes and juvenile detention centers. Assault and drug charges led to repeated imprisonments. In prison, he earned a reputation as a formidable boxer. His triumphs as a boxer earned him the nickname Lumberjack. His daily fitness routine boosted his self-esteem and gave him self-control.

Released at the age of 51, Robert had no job and no way to pay rent. He was homeless and hopeless. All he had was his daily exercise, which he did on a street corner in the Bronx.

A trip on the D train changed his life. The director of an independent film approached Robert. He was casting the role of a hardened ex-convict. Would he want to come to an audition? Hesitant at first, Robert went to the audition. He got the part.

Some of the filming took place on location at a prison in Long Island. One day, when Robert wasn't in a scene, he lay down in one of the cells for a nap. When he awoke, disoriented and confused, he forgot for a moment why he was there. He began to weep, believing he had once again been incarcerated.

Then he remembered the truth. He could open the door and simply walk out. He was free.[19]

It is amazing what the truth can do for a person.

For a moment, Robert believed the lie that he was in jail once again. His belief was based on his past history and experience.

Many Christians are believing lies that come from their past history and experiences. They have forgotten that Jesus came to open all the prison doors.

Believing lies about ourselves, about God, or even about how the world operates causes great pain, fear, and distress. Jesus came to set us free from the prison of sin. He also came to set us free from the lies that control our lives, steal our joy, and render us less effective for Him. Jesus reminded His followers: "Then you will know the truth, and the truth will set you free" (John 8:32).

When I spend time with young people, I often notice that their greatest distress comes from the lies they believe. They trust their first impressions of a situation and take their own thoughts as absolute truth.

No one likes me.

No one loves me.

Everyone abandons me.

Everyone else has friends but me.

God loves only perfect people.

I have to be perfect to gain my family's or friends' love.

I shouldn't have problems.

Things shouldn't be hard.

If people are angry with me, that means they don't love me.

I should get what I want. If I don't, terrible things will happen.

If people don't do what I want them to do, they must not love me.

I should make everyone happy all the time.

I am worse than other people. God will never be able to forgive me.

My worth and value is found in my grades, appearance, or achievements.

I have no future.

It is my fault.

These thoughts, which seem to be so automatic, start in childhood. It seems they come out of nowhere to ambush children. By the time they hit adolescence, unhappy teens have adopted these thoughts as part of their reality. These inaccurate ways of thinking can follow them into adulthood, creating anxiety, fear, and insecurity.

In 1987, at the signing of the Intermediate-range Nuclear Forces (INF) Treaty, President Ronald Reagan used the phrase "trust but verify" as a way of underscoring America's desire for the Soviet Union to commit to total compliance with the treaty. It has become a popular phrase for those working in foreign policy.

When it comes to our own internal thinking process, we are quick to trust but slow to verify. We assume that what we think and feel is accurate. We trust our own thoughts.

Maybe we shouldn't.

Speaking to the people of Israel, God said, "For my thoughts are not your thoughts, neither are your ways my ways" (Isaiah 55:8).

Challenging our own thoughts is a lot of work. It is even more difficult for young people. It certainly is easier to just believe what we are thinking, even if it causes misery. But it is worth the effort. Until we do the hard work of correcting our faulty beliefs, we will be imprisoned by our thoughts as surely as Robert was imprisoned by the steel bars of a prison cell.

Rather than trusting our own immediate thoughts, we can verify their accuracy or challenge their inaccuracy by looking at God's Word. We need to think His thoughts rather than our own.

Is it true that God loves only perfect people? Absolutely not. "But God demonstrates his own love for us in this: While we were still sinners, Christ died for us" (Romans 5:8).

Is it true that everyone abandons me? Not at all. "I am with you always, to the very end of the age" (Matthew 28:20).

Is it true that everyone will always reject me? Nope. "Whoever comes to me I will never drive away" (John 6:37).

Is it true that God can never forgive my sins? No way. " 'Come now, let us settle the matter,' says the LORD. 'Though your sins are like scarlet, they shall be as white as snow; though they are red as crimson, they shall be like wool' " (Isaiah 1:18).

Verify and trust.

Teach your grandchildren to first verify their thoughts by looking into God's Word. Then remind them to trust that what He says is true. Verify and then trust.

It is amazing what truth can do to set a person free.

Let Us Pray That . . .

- our grandchildren bring their thoughts captive to Jesus Christ (2 Corinthians 10:5).
- our grandchildren's minds will be renewed by the reading of God's Word (Romans 12:2).
- our grandchildren think about what is true (Philippians 4:8).
- our grandchildren grasp the truth that nothing will ever separate them from God's love (Romans 8:39).
- our grandchildren will be sanctified by the truth of God's Word (John 17:17).
- our grandchildren put on truth as part of their Christian armor (Ephesians 6:14).
- our grandchildren rely on the Holy Spirit to guide them to spiritual truth (John 16:13).

Lord, you are the Way, the Truth, and the Life. There is nothing like the freedom we have when we finally submit to your truth. Because of the truth of the gospel, we are free to love you and others without fear. Give our grandchildren the courage and wisdom to challenge their own thinking. Help them to understand that their thoughts are not always your thoughts. Renew their minds with the truth of your Word so they can live like the free people Jesus died for them to be. Amen.

Think and Do

- Looking for some help in identifying inaccurate or unbiblical thinking? For more than twenty years, Chris Thurman's book *The Lies We Believe* has helped many people as they struggle with faulty thinking. *Lies Women Believe: And the Truth that Sets Them Free* by Nancy Leigh DeMoss is another helpful resource.

- *Edwurd Fudwupper Fibbed Big* by Berkeley Breathed tells the story of Edwurd, who tells little fibs that grow into the biggest fib of all—with disastrous results. It's a fun book to read with kids if you want to have a general discussion about truth.

- Just before He was betrayed, Jesus prayed for His disciples in John 17:17, "Sanctify them by the truth; your word is truth." It was the desire of Jesus that His disciples be made holy and set apart by knowing the truth. That is His desire for each of us today. What is your next step in this process of sanctification?

"We demolish arguments and every pretension that sets itself up against the knowledge of God, and we take captive every thought to make it obedient to Christ" (2 Corinthians 10:5).

"Do not conform to the pattern of this world, but be transformed by the renewing of your mind. Then you will be able to test and approve what God's will is—his good, pleasing and perfect will" (Romans 12:2).

"Finally, brothers and sisters, whatever is true, whatever is noble, whatever is right, whatever is pure, whatever is lovely, whatever is admirable—if anything is excellent or praiseworthy—think about such things" (Philippians 4:8).

"Neither height nor depth, nor anything else in all creation, will be able to separate us from the love of God that is in Christ Jesus our Lord" (Romans 8:39).

"Sanctify them by the truth; your word is truth" (John 17:17).

"Stand firm then, with the belt of truth buckled around your waist, with the breastplate of righteousness in place" (Ephesians 6:14).

"But when he, the Spirit of truth, comes, he will guide you into all the truth. He will not speak on his own; he will speak only what he hears, and he will tell you what is yet to come" (John 16:13).

day fifty-eight:
LEGAL OR RIGHT?

It is better to be divided by truth than to be united in error. It is better to speak the truth that hurts and then heals, than falsehood that comforts and then kills.

Adrian Rogers

You are righteous, Lord, and your laws are right.
Psalm 119:137

Having been now separated from their grandchildren by nearly two thousand miles, Kelsie and Jerry were delighted to gather around the kitchen table in their daughter's home. The three grandkids were equally thrilled to have their proud grandma and grandpa on hand to listen to their jumble of stories about school, sports, church, friends, and dreams for the future.

Our friends' grandchildren are well-grounded and aware teens. Occasionally, comments about world events or an issue currently in the news would be scattered in among the details of homecoming or a football game.

Not wanting to stop the flow of conversation, Kelsie briefly cut in to ask her soon-to-be-adult grandkids, "You do know, don't you, that just because something is legal it doesn't make it right?"

What a wise grandma.

It is true. Making something legal doesn't make it right.

There have been behaviors throughout history that have been legal but not right.

In the 1930s and 1940s, the Nuremberg Laws made it permissible to exclude Jews from German citizenship, professions, and many areas of public life. Was it legal? Yes. Was it right? No.

Slavery as a lawful institution existed in the United States until 1865. Was it legal? Yes. Was it right? No.

In the 1973 landmark *Roe v. Wade* case, the Supreme Court of the United States ruled that abortion should be available. Is abortion legal? Yes. Is it right? No.

Some feel less guilt or stigma when certain behaviors are legalized. It helps them rationalize and minimize the consequences of their actions.

Megan was a beautiful young lady. She was intelligent, creative, and had the most likable personality. She frequently used marijuana. She admitted that she was unable to enjoy an evening with friends unless she was using. It was also obvious that her motivation and self-esteem had gone up in smoke. Her ability to enjoy everyday life was gone. When a friend encouraged her to stop, she replied, "Well, marijuana will be legal in some states soon."

I doubt the fact that marijuana is now legal in some states will ever give Megan back the time and money she has wasted. Making it legal doesn't make it right. It just made it easier for her to put off what she needed to do.

When faced with the decision about whether something is right or wrong, the question that needs to be answered is not "Is it legal?" Rather, we need to ask ourselves "What does God's Word say?"

The writer of Proverbs got straight to the point on this topic. He understood that many people make their decisions based on their own foolish opinions. He warned his son, "There is a way that appears to be right, but in the end it leads to death" (Proverbs 14:12).

This Old Testament book contains numerous weighty instructions about how to live a righteous life—a life where what is right before God is more important than what the world thinks. Over and over again, Solomon gives his son the same instructions:

Get wisdom.

Fear the Lord and gain knowledge and understanding.

Turn your ears to hear wisdom.

Pursue wisdom no matter what it costs.

Don't let wisdom out of your sight.

Delight in wisdom.

Remember that it is the Lord who gives wisdom.

In a world where what is legal is more important than what is right, our grandchildren are going to need the wisdom that only the Lord can give. I pray that our grandchildren will develop the thinking skills that will help them to not just accept the world's opinion about right and wrong.

May they give all that they have to obtain the wisdom that comes from knowing God and His Word.

Let Us Pray That . . .

- our grandchildren express their love for God through obedience to His commands (John 14:15).

- our grandchildren will have the boldness to obey God rather than man (Acts 5:29).

- our grandchildren will not be overwhelmed by evil but will overcome evil with good (Romans 12:21).

- our grandchildren will not neglect doing the good they know to do (James 4:17).

- our grandchildren show evidence of their relationship with God by obeying his commands (1 John 3:24).

Gracious Lord, you are the source of all wisdom. You know our need for sound judgment and have provided your Word to guide us. We pray for our grandchildren. May they be a generation that pursues wisdom. Lead them in your righteous ways. Give them the courage to stand for what is right even when all around them choose another path. May they receive the blessings you have promised as they pursue a deeper relationship with you. Give them great wisdom, Lord. Amen.

Think and Do

- Read Isaiah 5:20. Do you see any indication that our world is calling evil good and good evil? Taking a stand for what is right is critical.
- Do you ever know what is right to do but have difficulty doing it? Meditate on James 4:17 and pray for the strength to do what is right.
- Set aside time to pray for your grandchildren's parents as they guide their children through the murky waters of right and wrong.

"If you love me, keep my commands" (John 14:15).

"Peter and the other apostles replied: 'We must obey God rather than human beings!' " (Acts 5:29).

"The one who keeps God's commands lives in him, and he in them. And this is how we know that he lives in us: We know it by the Spirit he gave us" (1 John 3:24).

"Do not be overcome by evil, but overcome evil with good" (Romans 12:21).

"If anyone, then, knows the good they ought to do and doesn't do it, it is sin for them" (James 4:17).

day fifty-nine:
WINDOWS AND MIRRORS

Know thyself.

Plato

Anyone who listens to the word but does not do what it says is like someone who looks at his face in a mirror and, after looking at himself, goes away and immediately forgets what he looks like.

James 1:23–24

Laundry flapped in the wind on the clothesline. Gray, weather-beaten stones led to a garden filled with gladioli, tea roses, and bearded irises. Far off, green hills tumbled one into another. A red barn sat atop one hill like a crown.

In contrast to the lavish scene I viewed from her bedroom window, Grandma's room itself held the barest necessities. Strategically placed braided rugs protected hardwood floors. A white chenille bedspread was draped loosely over the sagging mattress on the tarnished brass bed.

The simple metal pulls on the mahogany dresser made a comforting rat-a-tat-tat sound each time Grandma opened and closed a drawer. Crocheted doilies marked the resting place of the only four items ever found atop the dresser: a picture of my mother at the age of two, an ancient hairbrush with soft bristles, a glass jar with hair pins, and a matching hand mirror that Grandmother never used. It was little wonder, since crackly lines and cloudy patches marred the deteriorated, formerly shiny coating—distorting any reflection. Still, it kept its honored place on the dresser.

Grandmother's mirror intrigued me. Recalling pictures of my grandmother as a young woman, I imagined that the petite, dark-haired girl might have used the mirror to put on lipstick for a party or to check the position of a silver hair comb.

Windows and mirrors both offer us unique views—of the world and of ourselves.

In his book *Good to Great,* author Jim Collins says that great leaders need to make appropriate use of both windows and mirrors. Collins believes that when things are going well, great leaders regularly look out the window, scanning the horizon for whom they can thank, acknowledge, recognize, or affirm. When things are not going well, they humbly pick up a mirror and engage in rigorous self-examination long before they examine anyone else.

Collins' principles not only make good business sense but (whether he knows it or not) they are also biblical—and result in spiritual, emotional, and relational health. The windows and mirrors concept is great advice for families.[20]

Facing difficulties, frustration, or pain, we frequently push back the curtains and scan the horizon for somewhere to place blame. Even worse, sometimes we open the window and hurl accusations at the unsuspecting people below.

The words of Jesus in Matthew 7:3–4 don't absolve others of their personal responsibility for their words or actions toward us. At the same time, they do plainly state that before we address another's sins, we must address our own: "Why worry about a speck in your friend's eye when you have a log in your own? How can you think of saying to your friend, 'Let me help you get rid of that speck in your eye,' when you can't see past the log in your own eye?" (NLT).

A ruthless personal humility is necessary to do this kind of self-examination. That our own tendency to sin is as great as any other person's is a frightening admission. What will people think if we admit we aren't perfect? Will we lose face with family, friends, and fellow Christians? After all, don't segments of the Christian culture send the message that perfection is within our reach?

To protect ourselves, we get busy with keeping up appearances through blaming others and ignoring our contribution to the relational quagmires of our lives.

Paul provides insight in his writing to the Romans as "loved by God and called to be his holy people" (1:7). He states, "For at whatever point you judge another, you are condemning yourself, because you who pass judgment do the same things" (2:1).

As I criticize another for being unkind, I must remember the harsh words said to my grandson when he spilled his milk. When I tell another about a sister's sin of gossip, I engage in the very thing I condemn. When I judge another for being unloving, I would do well to admit my own thoughtlessness and neglect toward others—perhaps a new widow, a hurting mom, or my own family.

Nowhere is our propensity to blame more lethal than in the home. The tendency to ignore one's own contribution to problems and to hurl accusations of blame at one's spouse has executed more marriages than adultery.

Grandma needed a new mirror because hers was distorted and foggy. The way we see ourselves is often just as blurred by fear and clouded by pride. We need the accurate reflections that can be provided for us by the Word of God and by honest Christian friends.

While it is painful to look at ourselves and admit our part when things aren't going well, it is also healthy and freeing. No one expresses this more clearly than Philip Yancey. "Imperfection is the prerequisite for grace. Light only gets in through the cracks."

When we admit the cracks in our own perfection, we allow grace to come in and do its work. Spiritually, we experience the relief of confessed sin and God's limitless forgiveness. Emotionally, we escape the hard work required to maintain self-deception. Relationally, we rush to push back the curtains of our lives and scan the horizon for people not to blame, but to bless and to love.

I have personally witnessed the damage caused by refusing to look at one's own sin. I have seen those who have opened the window and scanned the horizon, desperate for someone to blame so they could avoid taking responsibility. It never ends well.

My prayer is that my grandchildren will make appropriate use of both mirrors and windows. May they look in the mirror to engage in healthy self-examination. And may they throw open the window of their lives to shout words of affirmation, encouragement, and blessing to all in their view. I pray that they will experience spiritual, emotional, and relational health as they respond with maturity to life's challenges.

Let Us Pray That . . .

- our grandchildren look into the mirror of God's Word and never forget its teaching (James 1:23–25).

- our grandchildren will not consider themselves as better than others but will judge themselves with honesty and humility (Romans 12:3; Galatians 6:3–5).

- our grandchildren confess their sins and failings, and find forgiveness through Jesus Christ (1 John 1:9).

- our grandchildren reject the world's message of perfection and see their own imperfections as opportunities to experience the grace of God (2 Corinthians 12:9).

- our grandchildren use their words not to blame others but to bless and build up (Ephesians 4:29).

- our grandchildren become mature and complete in Christ Jesus (Ephesians 4:15).

Heavenly Father, I confess my own tendency to avoid taking responsibility for relational problems. I become laser focused on another person's faults, and I ignore my own. Help me to embrace the truth found in Jesus' words in Matthew 7 and to humbly look for the logs in my own life. Lord, I long for my grandchildren to have healthy relationships. Teach them to take responsibility for their own words, thoughts, and actions. May they learn to look for ways to encourage and affirm others. I know that this pattern—taking responsibility for our own sin and extending grace to other people—is the prescription for happy homes and friendships. I thank you for the truth of your Word. Amen.

Think and Do

- Look into the mirror of Colossians 3:12–15. What can you change in your interactions with family and friends? How can you take responsibility for any breakdown in communication or respect?

- "As long as you are proud you cannot know God. A proud man is always looking down on things and people: and, of course, as long as you are looking down you cannot see something that is above you" (C. S. Lewis, *Mere Christianity*). How does our negative and blaming view of other people obstruct our view of God?

- Self-examination and self-loathing are two different things. Self-examination leads to godly sorrow, which leads to life (2 Corinthians 7:10). Self-loathing is a dead-end street. Self-loathing often leads to self-pity. Both still have "self" at the center. Neither allows us to achieve our goal of loving God and loving others. How do you think we can avoid this pitfall? Read 1 Corinthians 16:14.

"Anyone who listens to the word but does not do what it says is like someone who looks at his face in a mirror and, after looking at himself, goes away and immediately forgets what he looks like. But whoever looks intently into the perfect law that gives freedom, and continues in it—not forgetting what they have heard, but doing it—they will be blessed in what they do" (James 1:23–25).

"If anyone thinks they are something when they are not, they deceive themselves. Each one should test their own actions. Then they can take pride in themselves alone, without comparing themselves to someone else, for each one should carry their own load" (Galatians 6:3–5).

"If we confess our sins, he is faithful and just and will forgive us our sins and purify us from all unrighteousness" (1 John 1:9).

"But he said to me, 'My grace is sufficient for you, for my power is made perfect in weakness.' Therefore I will boast all the more gladly about my weaknesses, so that Christ's power may rest on me" (2 Corinthians 12:9).

"Do not let any unwholesome talk come out of your mouths, but only what is helpful for building others up according to their needs, that it may benefit those who listen" (Ephesians 4:29).

"Instead, speaking the truth in love, we will grow to become in every respect the mature body of him who is the head, that is, Christ" (Ephesians 4:15).

"For by the grace given me I say to every one of you: Do not think of yourself more highly than you ought, but rather think of yourself with sober judgment, in accordance with the faith God has distributed to each of you" (Romans 12:3).

day sixty:
GO TO YOUR HAPPY PLACE

If God be our God, He will give us peace in trouble. When there is a storm without, He will make peace within. The world can create trouble in peace, but God can create peace in trouble.

Thomas Watson

You will keep in perfect peace those whose minds are steadfast, because they trust in you.

Isaiah 26:3

The Black Forest in southwestern Germany is my favorite place on earth.

After visiting Strasbourg, our family had an appointment at Black Forest Academy in Kandern. The one-hour trip took us briefly through the countryside of Alsace-Lorraine. Hundreds of round hay bales dotted serene and gently rolling farmland. Cows, sheep, and goats grazed close to the road, undisturbed by passing cars.

After our visit to the Academy, we decided to continue on the A5 deeper into the Black Forest. We were headed for the German village of Titisee.

Narrow but well cared for roads twisted and turned as the terrain grew steeper. Millions of evergreens covered the mountainside. Crystal clear, ice-cold streams ran alongside the road. With dark rock and thousands of pines on each side, our car was sheltered with a canopy of darkness. The forest truly looked black.

We were in the clock-making part of Germany, and I imagined lederhosen-clad woodcutters and skillful carvers working

272

away, wood chips flying, in tiny cottages deep in the enchanted forest. Their wives were baking strudel.

After an hour of the cool, quiet shadows of the Black Forest, we drove around a curve to witness the stunning view of the placid Lake Titisee. Before us was the picturesque mountain village, complete with tile-roofed houses and shops. It was all you would hope for in a German village.

It was peaceful.

If I am ever told to go to my happy place, that is where you will probably find me—in the Black Forest eating a piece of cherry *gateaux*.

Some people use their "happy place" as a way of reducing stress and anxiety and finding moments of peace. Dreaming of the Black Forest can bring warm memories to mind and a smile to my face. However, it does little for my stress and anxiety.

I have another happy place. I should go there more often.

The apostle Paul tells us about it: "Do not be anxious about anything, but in every situation, by prayer and petition, with thanksgiving, present your requests to God. And the peace of God, which transcends all understanding, will guard your hearts and your minds in Christ Jesus" (Philippians 4:6–7).

I am often anxious about my children's and my grandchildren's needs. Nighttime worrying has cost me untold hours of sleeplessness and solved nothing. I am slowly learning what I need to do to find peace when fear ensnares me in the wee hours of the morning.

I need to go to Jesus. He is my place of peace.

I can bring my request to Him and not only pray for the specific need but also remind myself of what God wants to do. I try to focus my heart and mind on the big picture of God's work. Somehow, remembering important Scriptures about God's agenda calms me and allows me to regain a proper perspective.

Choosing key words from verses and arranging them in a way I can remember, even in the darkness, has allowed me to rest and find peace in God's presence.

Just before departing this earth for heaven, Jesus promised to His disciples His unique peace. He instructed them to trust—not to be troubled.

If we take Him at His word, we can be sure that He means for our hearts to be at rest as we trust in Him.

When I bring my concerns to Jesus, I truly have found the happy place that relieves my stress and anxiety.

Let Us Pray That . . .

- our grandchildren find peace as they discover how the following words can be applied to their lives:

Acknowledge—Acknowledge God in all of their ways (Proverbs 3:5–6).

Believe—Believe in Jesus even though they have not seen Him—yet are blessed by believing (John 20:29).

Care—Remember and trust that God cares so much that they can give their concerns to Him (1 Peter 5:7).

Delight—Delight in God and be totally satisfied with His love (Psalm 37:4).

Everlasting—Find refuge in God and believe that His everlasting arms are always ready to catch them (Deuteronomy 33:27).

Father—Enjoy an intimate relationship with our heavenly Father (Matthew 6:9).

Good—Believe that God always fulfills all of His good promises (Joshua 21:45).

Hope—Hope in their Savior all the day long (Psalm 25:5).

Infinite—Accept and enjoy God's infinite love (Psalm 103: 11).

Joy—Believe in Jesus and experience inexpressible joy (1 Peter 1:8).

Know—Take time to be still and truly know God (Psalm 46:10).

Love—Love the Lord God with all their heart and love their neighbors as themselves (Matthew 22:37).

Mercy—Show mercy to all people (Matthew 5:7).

Nothing—Believe and live out the truth that nothing can separate them from the love of God (Romans 8:31–39).

Open—Open the door of their lives to Jesus and allow Him to have control of every area (Revelation 3:20).

Please—Make their first priority pleasing God (2 Corinthians 5:9).

Quiet—Closely follow the Shepherd to the quiet waters (Psalm 23:2).

Redeemer—Remember that their Redeemer lives (Job 19:25).

Strength—Trust in the Lord and find strength in Him (Psalm 28:7).

Truth—Find freedom in the truth of the gospel (John 14:6).

Unfailing—Trust in God's unfailing love (Psalm 13:5).

Victory—Experience victory through the Lord Jesus Christ (1 Corinthians 15:57).

Worship—Worship in spirit and truth (John 4:23).

Prince of Peace, I find my rest in you. I thank you that you are able to give peace in a way that the world never could. I thank you for the certainty that you care for my grandchildren and are able to meet every need. When I consider your promises, I am filled to overflowing with your peace. Lord, I pray that my grandchildren will find the tranquility that comes from staying close to you and remaining focused on you. When they are tempted to find peace elsewhere, may they be restless until they come to you once again. Help them to take you at your word, that you are the one who gives lasting peace. May their minds be fixed on you so they can experience perfect peace as you have promised. Amen.

Think and Do

- Read Isaiah 9:6; Luke 2:14; John 20:26; Ephesians 2:14. What does each verse teach you about Jesus and peace? What do you think the implications are of Jesus being the Prince of Peace? How does this apply to your prayer life?

- Have you found an effective strategy to regain your spiritual peace when life is chaotic? How do you find a peaceful place when you are concerned about your grandchildren?

- May you experience more and more the peace of God as you replace anxiety with prayer.

NOTES

Chapter Two

1. Kathryn Stockett, *The Help* (New York: Amy Einhorn Books Putnam, 2009), 443.

2. John Trent and Gary Smalley, *The Blessing* (Nashville: Thomas Nelson, 1987), 29.

Chapter Three

3. Roger Olson, "Did Karl Barth Really Say, 'Jesus Loves Me, This I Know'?" Patheos.com, January 24, 2013, http://www.patheos.com/blogs/rogereolson/2013/01 /did-karl-barth-really-say-jesus-loves-me-this-i-know/.

Chapter Six

4. Max Lucado, *And the Angels Were Silent: Walking with Christ Toward the Cross* (Nashville: Thomas Nelson, 1987), 29.

Chapter Eight

5. Bruce Winston, "Quality and Quantity of Work" devotional from *Be a Leader for God's Sake* website (www.bealeaderforgodssake.org). Used with permission.

Chapter Nine

6. Billy Graham, "The Need for Love," *Billy Graham Evangelistic Association*, May 5, 2014, www.billygraham.org/devotion /the-need-for-love/.

7. Susan Bosak, "Why Grandparents are VIPs," *The Legacy Project*, www.legacyproject.org/guides/gpvip.html.

8. Peter Scazzero, *The Emotionally Healthy Church* (Grand Rapids: Zondervan, 2003), 10.

Chapter Twenty-two

9. Ralph C. Wood, *The Gospel According to Tolkien* (Louisville: Westminster John Knox Press, 2003), 24.

Chapter Thirty

10. C. S. Lewis, *The Weight of Glory* (New York: Harper Collins Publishers, 2001), 187.

Chapter Thirty-five

11. David Harding, "Stranger Moves Into Family's Home," *Daily News*, November 30, 2013, www.nydailynews.com/life-style /real-estate/stranger-takes-family-home-legal-article-1.1533414.

Chapter Thirty-seven

12. "St. Cloud Man Dies after Injuries from Punch," *CBS Minnesota*, September 22, 2012, minnesota.cbslocal.com/2012/09/22 /st-cloud-man-dies-after-random-punch/.

Chapter Forty

13. Tony Reinke, "Ian and Larissa: One Year Later," *Desiring God*, May 8, 2013, www.desiringgod.org/blog/posts/ian-and -larissa-one-year-later.

Chapter Forty-one

14. Philip Gulley, *Front Porch Tales* (San Francisco: HarperOne, 2007), 150.

Chapter Forty-two

15. Everett Worthington, *Dimensions of Forgiveness: Psychological Research and Theological Perspectives* (West Conshohocken, PA: Templeton Foundation Press, 1998), 108.

Chapter Fifty-two

16. "Good King Wenceslas," *Storynory*, www.storynory.com /2010/12/13/king-wenceslas.

17. C. S. Lewis, *Mere Christianity* (New York: Harper Collins, 2007), 77.

Chapter Fifty-four

18. Gail Godwin, *Heart* (New York: Bloomsbury, 2004), 5.

Chapter Fifty-seven

19. Corey Kilgannon, "Sidewalk Is His Prison Yard," *New York Times*, March 1, 2011, nytimes.com/2011/03/13/nyregion/13sweat .html?_r=0.

Chapter Fifty-nine

20. Jim Collins, *Good to Great* (New York: Harper Collins, 2001), 33.

NOTE TO THE READER

The publisher invites you to share your response to the message of this book by writing Discovery House Publishers, P.O. Box 3566, Grand Rapids, MI 49501, U.S.A. For information about other Discovery House books, music, or DVDs, contact us at the same address or call 1-800-653-8333. Find us on the Internet at dhp.org or send e-mail to books@dhp.org.

ABOUT THE AUTHOR

Kay Swatkowski is a pastoral counselor licensed by the National Christian Counselors Association and ministering through North Point Church in Winthrop Harbor, Illinois. Kay is also a speaker and writer, focusing her passion on a variety of issues related to families and spiritual direction. She has previously worked as a Christian schoolteacher, women's ministry director for Converge MidAmerica, and children's ministry director for Faith Church in Grayslake, Illinois. Kay and her husband of forty years, Ray, have been involved in church planting in the United States, and they spent three years serving as missionaries to France. Presently Ray ministers through Pinnacle Ministries in Mosinee, Wisconsin. The Swatkowskis have four children and five grandchildren. They reside in Antioch, Illinois, only twenty minutes away from all of the grandkids.